SpringerBriefs in Offending Populations & Correctional Psychotherapy

Series Editor

Karla Sapp, Midway, GA, USA

SpringerBriefs in Offending Populations & Correctional Psychotherapy is a series of compact, high-quality volumes dealing with all aspects of the American carceral system and offender populations, from identifying systemic issues of the prison system to addressing services needed to support offender mental health.

Featuring concise titles between 50-125 pages, the cross-disciplinary series incorporates research and policy suggestions spanning mental health, criminal justice, and more, including topics such as correctional psychology and counseling, transformative and restorative justice, recidivism and rehabilitation, advocacy and public policy issues, and dismantling prison pipelines.

SpringerBriefs in Offending Populations & Correctional Psychotherapy will be of interest to a broad range of researchers and practitioners working in offender and prison research and in related academic fields such as Psychology, Counseling, Criminology, Criminal Justice, and Law.

Karla Sapp

Exploring Developmental Trauma Disorder Among Offending Populations

In Pursuit of Healing and Justice

Springer

Karla Sapp
Project Hope
Midway, GA, USA

ISSN 2731-8966 ISSN 2731-8974 (electronic)
SpringerBriefs in Offending Populations & Correctional Psychotherapy
ISBN 978-3-031-61156-8 ISBN 978-3-031-61157-5 (eBook)
https://doi.org/10.1007/978-3-031-61157-5

This Springer imprint is published by the registered company Springer Nature Switzerland AG
The registered company address is: Gewerbestrasse 11, 6330 Cham, Switzerland

Preface

In the vast landscape of the criminal justice system, a hidden crisis lurks beneath the surface, one that remains largely unnoticed and inadequately addressed—the prevalence of Developmental Trauma Disorder among offending populations. This book, *Exploring Developmental Trauma Disorder Among Offending Populations: In Pursuit of Healing and Justice*, sheds light on a silent epidemic that has long been ignored by the justice system, offering a comprehensive examination of the impact of developmental trauma on individuals involved in criminal behavior.

Through a deep dive into the prevalence and characteristics of developmental trauma among offending populations, this book uncovers the profound attachment difficulties, emotional dysregulation, and impaired social functioning that characterize this often-unrecognized disorder. By exploring the unique challenges faced by individuals with developmental trauma within the justice system, we aim to bring awareness to the complexities of their experiences and the urgent need for targeted interventions and support mechanisms.

Central to our exploration is the intricate cycle of developmental trauma and criminal behavior, where unresolved trauma begets maladaptive coping strategies, perpetuating a cycle of reoffending. By tracing the interplay between trauma and criminality, we illuminate the pathways through which trauma manifests in offending behavior and highlight the necessity of addressing these root causes for effective rehabilitation and reintegration.

Furthermore, this book delves into the transformative potential of trauma-informed approaches within the criminal justice system, emphasizing the critical importance of creating safe, supportive environments that recognize and respond to the impact of trauma on behavior. By advocating for trauma-informed care, training for justice system personnel, and trauma screening tools, we strive to promote a more compassionate and effective response to individuals with developmental trauma involved in offending behavior.

In exploring interventions for healing and recovery among offenders with developmental trauma, this book delves into evidence-based practices, trauma-focused therapy, and skill-building programs aimed at promoting resilience and fostering positive social connections. By highlighting the power of comprehensive, integrated interventions, we seek to empower individuals to address the underlying trauma that drives their behavior and embark on a path towards healing and recovery.

Finally, this book delves into the policy implications and recommendations necessary for effecting systemic change within the criminal justice system. By advocating for trauma-informed approaches, increased access to mental health services, and policy reforms that prioritize trauma-specific interventions, we aim to pave the way for a more rehabilitative, supportive, and equitable justice system that upholds the dignity and well-being of individuals impacted by developmental trauma.

As we embark on this journey of exploration, reflection, and advocacy, we invite you to delve into the complexities of Developmental Trauma Disorder among offending populations and join us in the call for transformative actions that promote healing, rehabilitation, and resilience within the criminal justice system. Together, let us work toward a more just, compassionate, and supportive future for all individuals impacted by developmental trauma.

Midway, GA, USA Karla Sapp

Acknowledgments

I would like to express my deepest gratitude to all those who have contributed to the creation of *Exploring Developmental Trauma Disorder Among Offending Populations: In Pursuit of Healing and Justice*.

First and foremost, I extend my sincere appreciation to the individuals within the criminal justice system who have shared their invaluable experiences, perspectives, and knowledge. Their willingness to open up and offer insights into the complexities of offending behavior has been instrumental in shaping the content of this brief.

I am immensely grateful to the numerous researchers and experts in the fields of criminology, psychology, and correctional psychotherapy whose work has provided the foundation for this book. Their groundbreaking research, innovative theories, and evidence-based practices have guided and informed the discussions throughout the chapters.

I owe a profound debt of gratitude to the clinicians, therapists, and mental health professionals who work tirelessly within correctional settings. Their dedication, compassion, and unwavering commitment to supporting offender rehabilitation have been a true inspiration. I am humbled by their resilience, resourcefulness, and the transformative impact they make in the lives of individuals under their care.

I would also like to acknowledge the support and encouragement of my colleagues and peers, who have provided valuable insights and feedback throughout the writing process. Your guidance and collaboration have been instrumental in shaping this book and enhancing its overall quality.

My heartfelt thanks go to the editorial and publishing team for their expertise, professionalism, and continuous support in bringing this brief to life. Your meticulous attention to detail and unwavering belief in the importance of disseminating knowledge in this field have been truly commendable.

Finally, I am eternally grateful to my family, friends, and loved ones for their unwavering support, understanding, and encouragement throughout this endeavor. Your belief in me and your unwavering encouragement has been the cornerstone of my journey. To my Daddy who is now my Angel in Heaven, I am forever grateful for your steadfast support throughout the years and continuous beliefs and pride in me! I AM because of You and Momma!!!!!

To all those mentioned and the countless others who have in some way contributed to this book, I offer my sincerest gratitude. It is with great pleasure and gratitude that I present *Exploring Developmental Trauma Disorder Among Offending Populations: In Pursuit of Healing and Justice* to the readers, hoping it will inspire meaningful dialogue, innovative practices, and positive change in the field of offender rehabilitation.

Contents

Chapter 1
Shattering the Silence – An Introduction to Exploring Developmental Trauma Among Offending Populations

1.1 The Silent Epidemic Ignored by the Justice System

The justice system plays a vital role in maintaining law and order while addressing the needs of offenders. However, in its pursuit of punishment and rehabilitation, the justice system often overlooks the presence and implications of developmental trauma within offending populations. This oversight can be attributed to a lack of understanding and recognition of the prevalence and impact of developmental trauma on the lives of those who engage in criminal behavior.

Sadly, developmental trauma remains a largely unaddressed silent epidemic within the justice system. Astonishingly, up to 90% of incarcerated individuals have experienced some form of childhood trauma (Dvoskin et al., 2020). However, this crucial aspect of an offender's life is often dismissed or overshadowed by the focus on the offense committed, thereby perpetuating a cycle of reoffending and hindering opportunities for authentic healing and successful rehabilitation.

Developmental trauma refers to adverse experiences occurring during critical periods of brain development that can have profound and lasting impacts on an individual's psychological, social, and emotional well-being (van der Kolk, 2009). These traumatic experiences, which include neglect, abuse, violence, and chronic instability, contribute to maladaptive coping strategies and an increased likelihood of engaging in criminal behavior (Ford et al., 2013). However, the recognition and understanding of developmental trauma within the justice system remains limited.

K. Sapp, *Exploring Developmental Trauma Disorder Among Offending Populations*, SpringerBriefs in Offending Populations & Correctional Psychotherapy,
https://doi.org/10.1007/978-3-031-61157-5_1

1.2 The Significance of Recognizing and Addressing Developmental Trauma

Recognizing and addressing developmental trauma among offenders is of utmost significance for several reasons. Firstly, research consistently demonstrates that a substantial number of individuals involved in the justice system have experienced significant trauma during their childhood and adolescence (Stensrud et al., 2019). The prevalence of developmental trauma within offender populations underscores its relevance and importance within the context of criminal behavior.

Furthermore, unresolved developmental trauma perpetuates a cycle of offending and victimization, leading to high rates of recidivism. The justice system traditionally focuses on punishment rather than addressing the underlying causes of criminal behavior, including trauma (Covington & Bloom, 2003). By neglecting the psychological and emotional needs of offenders with developmental trauma, the system misses crucial opportunities for rehabilitation and fails to break the cycle of reoffending.

Failure to recognize and address developmental trauma also undermines principles of equity and fairness within the justice system. Offenders who have experienced trauma often face multiple disadvantages, such as limited access to resources and socioeconomic challenges, which compound their involvement in criminal behavior (Suonpää et al., 2018). Ignoring the traumatic backgrounds of offenders perpetuates systemic inequalities and hampers their chances of successful reintegration into society.

1.3 The Objectives of the Book

The objective of this book is to explore the multifaceted aspects of developmental trauma within offending populations and provide a comprehensive understanding of its effects on individuals and society. By examining current research, sharing case studies, and highlighting trauma-informed approaches, I aim to:

- Increase awareness and understanding of developmental trauma among professionals within the criminal justice system (Stensrud et al., 2019). Through collaboration between trauma and criminal justice fields, we can work towards developing interdisciplinary approaches that address the complex needs of offenders with developmental trauma.
- Seeks to advocate for trauma-informed policies and practices within correctional institutions, community-based programs, and aftercare services. By recognizing the impact of developmental trauma and implementing trauma-informed care, we can provide opportunities for healing and rehabilitation, ultimately reducing recidivism rates and improving outcomes for individuals with a history of trauma.

- Equip mental health professionals in the criminal justice system with evidence-based interventions and services that specifically address the underlying developmental trauma impacting criminal behavior. By enhancing the knowledge base of these professionals, we can empower them to provide effective trauma-informed interventions to offenders.

1.4 Conclusion

In conclusion, this book aims to shine a light on the silent epidemic of developmental trauma within offending populations, ultimately advocating for a more compassionate, effective, and just approach to offender rehabilitation. Through increased awareness, the promotion of trauma-informed practices, and policy changes within the justice system, we can address the profound impact of developmental trauma and facilitate healing and growth among offenders.

References

Covington, S. S., & Bloom, B. E. (2003). Gendered justice: Women in the criminal justice system. In *Gendered justice: Addressing female offenders* (pp. 3–23). Carolina Academic Press.

Dvoskin, J. A., Knoll, J. L., & Silva, M. (2020). A brief history of the criminalization of mental illness. *CNS Spectrums, 25*(5), 638–650.

Ford, J. D., Grasso, D. J., Hawke, J., & Chapman, J. F. (2013). Poly-victimization among juvenile justice-involved youths. *Child Abuse & Neglect, 37*(10), 788–800.

Stensrud, R. H., Gilbride, D. D., & Bruinekool, R. M. (2019). The childhood to prison pipeline: Early childhood trauma as reported by a prison population. *Rehabilitation Counseling Bulletin, 62*(4), 195–208.

Suonpää, K., Kivivuori, J., & Aaltonen, M. (2018). Criminal history and social disadvantage as predictors of the severity of violent offending. *International Journal of Comparative and Applied Criminal Justice, 42*(2–3), 139–155.

Van der Kolk, B. A. (2009). Developmental trauma disorder: towards a rational diagnosis for chronically traumatized children. *Praxis der Kinderpsychologie und Kinderpsychiatrie, 58*(8), 572–586.

Chapter 2
Prevalence and Characteristics of Developmental Trauma Among Offenders

2.1 Prevalence Rates of Developmental Trauma Among Offending Populations

Research consistently indicates higher prevalence rates of developmental trauma among offending populations compared to the general population. Multiple studies have documented this association, providing valuable insights into the extent of the issue. For example, Coid et al. (2013) conducted a study involving women primary care attenders to assess the prevalence of abusive experiences and psychiatric morbidity. They found a high prevalence of developmental trauma among these women, with approximately 36% reporting childhood sexual abuse, 45% reporting emotional abuse, and 26% reporting physical abuse. These findings provide evidence of the high prevalence of developmental trauma experiences among individuals who later engage in criminal behavior.

Another study by Wrenn et al. (2011) explored the impact of trauma, including developmental trauma, on the quality of life of inner-city primary care patients. While this study does not focus solely on offenders, it highlights the prevalence of trauma exposure in a specific population. The findings indicated that 32% of the participants experienced moderate to severe traumatic events during childhood. Although not directly related to offending, this study underscores the importance of recognizing the prevalence of developmental trauma in various populations.

In a study by Ford et al. (2006), the authors examined the pathways from traumatic child victimization to delinquency, specifically focusing on the impact of trauma on specialized court proceedings. They found that individuals who had experienced childhood trauma had an increased likelihood of engaging in delinquent behavior that led to court involvement. This study supports the hypothesis that developmental trauma significantly contributes to offending behavior.

K. Sapp, *Exploring Developmental Trauma Disorder Among Offending Populations*, SpringerBriefs in Offending Populations & Correctional Psychotherapy, https://doi.org/10.1007/978-3-031-61157-5_2

Furthermore, a meta-analysis conducted by Maniglio (2015) examined the prevalence rates of childhood sexual abuse among delinquent individuals. The results indicated a significant association, with the prevalence of childhood sexual abuse being approximately 36% among delinquent individuals. This study offers further evidence of the high prevalence of developmental trauma in offending populations.

In conclusion, the findings consistently support the notion that individuals involved in criminal behavior have a higher prevalence of developmental trauma compared to the general population. Studies by Coid et al. (2013), Wrenn et al. (2011), Ford et al. (2006), and Maniglio (2015) provide valuable insights into this issue. Recognizing the high prevalence rates of developmental trauma among offenders is crucial in understanding the complex interplay between trauma and criminal behavior.

2.2 Long-Term Effects of Developmental Trauma

Developmental trauma can have severe and long-lasting effects on cognitive, emotional, and social functions. Cognitive impairments resulting from developmental trauma may include difficulties with attention, memory, and executive functioning (Teicher et al., 2006). Emotional dysregulation is a common consequence, leading to increased rates of anxiety, depression, and anger (Wrenn et al., 2011). Social impairments may manifest as difficulties forming and maintaining healthy relationships, poor impulse control, and interpersonal conflicts (Herman, 2015).

2.2.1 Cognitive Effects

Developmental trauma can have significant cognitive effects on individuals. Teicher et al. (2006) found that childhood trauma, including abuse and neglect, is associated with impairments in attention, memory, and executive functioning. These impairments can interfere with academic achievement, information processing, and decision-making abilities. The impact of developmental trauma on cognitive functioning may persist into adulthood, affecting an individual's daily functioning and overall quality of life.

Moreover, a study by Majer et al. (2010) examined the impact of childhood trauma on cognitive functioning in healthy adults residing in Wichita, Kansas. The findings revealed that individuals with a history of developmental trauma exhibited deficits in various cognitive domains, such as attention, memory, and executive functioning. These cognitive impairments may contribute to difficulties in maintaining employment, managing finances, and engaging in daily tasks.

2.2.2 Emotional Effects

The emotional consequences of developmental trauma are profound and can persist throughout an individual's life. Individuals who have experienced trauma during their childhood are at an increased risk of developing mental health disorders such as anxiety, depression, and post-traumatic stress disorder (PTSD) (Wrenn et al., 2011). These emotional disorders can significantly impact an individual's well-being, relationships, and overall quality of life.

Herman (2015) emphasizes that individuals who have experienced developmental trauma often struggle with emotional dysregulation. They may exhibit intense mood swings, impulsivity, and difficulty managing emotions. Emotional dysregulation can lead to challenges in forming and maintaining healthy relationships, as well as problems with self-esteem and self-worth. The emotional scars left by developmental trauma can undermine an individual's ability to cope with stress and adversity.

2.2.3 Social Effects

Developing secure attachments and forming healthy relationships can be challenging for individuals who have experienced developmental trauma. Abused and neglected children may struggle to trust others and may exhibit difficulties in establishing and maintaining meaningful connections (Herman, 2015). These social challenges can lead to social isolation, feelings of loneliness, and difficulties in developing a support network.

Furthermore, developmental trauma can contribute to challenges with impulse control and aggression (Wrenn et al., 2011). Individuals who have experienced trauma may engage in risky behaviors, exhibit anger management issues, and struggle with conflict resolution. These social difficulties can negatively impact an individual's educational attainment, employment opportunities, and overall social integration.

2.2.4 Conclusion

The long-term effects of developmental trauma are extensive and pervasive, impacting multiple aspects of an individual's life. Cognitive impairments, emotional dysregulation, and social difficulties are key consequences of developmental trauma. These effects can persist into adulthood, significantly affecting an individual's overall functioning and well-being. Recognizing and addressing the long-term effects of developmental trauma is crucial in providing appropriate support and interventions for those who have experienced such trauma.

2.3 Connection Between Developmental Trauma and Adverse Childhood Experiences (ACEs)

The connection between developmental trauma, adverse childhood experiences (ACES), and offending behavior is a complex and multifaceted topic. Adverse Childhood Experiences (ACEs) encompass a range of traumatic experiences, including abuse, neglect, and household dysfunction. Abuse, both physical and sexual, has been shown to have a significant impact on the development of developmental trauma and subsequent offending behavior (Briere & Elliott, 2003). Neglect, characterized by the absence of appropriate care, has also been strongly associated with developmental trauma and increases the risk of criminal involvement (Kendall-Tackett et al., 1993). Furthermore, growing up in environments characterized by household dysfunction, such as substance abuse, domestic violence, or mental illness, further intensifies the likelihood of experiencing developmental trauma and engaging in criminal behavior (Whitfield et al., 2003).

Research consistently shows that individuals who have experienced developmental trauma and a higher number of ACES have an increased risk of engaging in offending behavior (Fergusson et al., 2008). The connection between developmental trauma, ACES, and offending behavior can be understood through various mechanisms and pathways. For instance, Anda et al. (2006) conducted an influential study known as the Adverse Childhood Experiences (ACE) study, which examined the relationship between ACES and subsequent health and behavioral outcomes. The study revealed a strong association between ACES and negative behaviors, including criminal behavior. Individuals with a higher ACE score were found to be more likely to engage in delinquent activities, violent behavior, or criminal offenses. This study highlights the impact of adverse experiences during childhood on the development of problematic behaviors later in life.

Furthermore, a study by Ford et al. (2006) investigated the relationship between developmental trauma, ACES, and juvenile delinquency. The findings indicated that individuals who had greater exposure to ACES were more likely to exhibit higher rates of psychological symptoms and engage in delinquent behavior. The study suggests that developmental trauma experienced during childhood can contribute to the development of conduct problems and antisocial behaviors, leading to involvement in offending behavior. It is important to note that not all individuals who experience developmental trauma or ACES will engage in criminal behavior. However, the cumulative impact of these adverse experiences can significantly increase the likelihood of engaging in offending behavior.

The connection between developmental trauma, adverse childhood experiences (ACES), and offending behavior is evident from numerous research studies. The ACE study by Anda et al. (2006) and studies by Ford et al. (2006) highlight the association between ACES, developmental trauma, and subsequent involvement in delinquent and criminal activities. These studies contribute to our understanding of the complex interplay between traumatic experiences during childhood and the development of problematic behaviors later in life. Recognizing the link between developmental trauma, ACES, and offending behavior is crucial for implementing effective prevention, intervention, and treatment strategies. By addressing the underlying trauma and providing appropriate support and resources, we can work towards interrupting the cycle of trauma and criminal behavior, promoting healthier development and positive outcomes for individuals affected by ACES and developmental trauma.

2.3.1 *Key Points*

Key points focused on the connection between Developmental Trauma, Adverse Childhood Experiences (ACEs), and offending behaviors, includes:

1. Developmental trauma, which refers to chronic and prolonged stress experienced during sensitive periods of a child's development, can have lasting impacts on their well-being (Anda et al., 2006).
2. Adverse Childhood Experiences (ACEs) encompass various negative events or circumstances that children may encounter, such as abuse, neglect, or household dysfunction (Felitti et al., 1998).
3. There is a strong link between developmental trauma, ACEs, and engaging in offending behaviors. Studies have shown that individuals with higher ACE scores are at an increased risk of committing criminal offenses (Dierkhising et al., 2013).
4. Childhood trauma and ACEs can disrupt the normal development of brain regions involved in emotional regulation, impulse control, and decision-making, which can contribute to engagement in offending behaviors (Teicher et al., 2002).
5. The cumulative effects of multiple ACEs, especially when experienced during sensitive periods, can significantly increase the likelihood of engaging in criminal behavior later in life (Dong et al., 2005).
6. Developmental trauma and ACEs can lead to the development of maladaptive coping mechanisms, such as aggression, substance abuse, or delinquency, which serve as strategies to manage the psychological distress associated with trauma (Merrick et al., 2017).
7. The intergenerational transmission of trauma plays a role in the connection between developmental trauma, ACEs, and offending behaviors. Children who experience trauma or ACEs are more likely to perpetuate or be exposed to similar adverse experiences, further contributing to their involvement in criminal activities (Repetti et al., 2002).
8. Though not all individuals who experience developmental trauma or ACEs will engage in offending behaviors, the cumulative effects of these adversities increase the overall risk (Fox et al., 2015).
9. Early recognition and intervention are crucial in addressing the connection between developmental trauma, ACEs, and offending behaviors. Trauma-informed approaches, therapeutic interventions, and support systems can help mitigate the risk factors and promote positive outcomes (Ford et al., 2013).

2.4 Influence of Race, Ethnicity, and Socio-economic Factors

The relationship between developmental trauma and offending behaviors is influenced by various factors, including race, ethnicity, and socio-economic status. Research has shown that marginalized communities, often characterized by poverty and racial disparities, face higher rates of exposure to traumatic events (Fazel et al., 2008). Disparities in access to resources, such as mental health services and social support, may exacerbate the impact of trauma and increase the likelihood of involvement in criminal activities (Glaze & Maruschak, 2010). Moreover, the intersection of race and trauma is complex, with racial minority individuals often experiencing higher rates of trauma and facing additional barriers when seeking help or treatment (Williams et al., 2021). The overrepresentation of racial and ethnic minorities within the criminal justice system underscores the need for a more comprehensive understanding of the influence of race, ethnicity, and socio-economic factors on the relationship between trauma and offending.

2.4.1 Race and Ethnicity

Research suggests that race and ethnicity significantly impact the relationship between developmental trauma and offending behaviors. Multiple studies have shown disparities in how race and ethnicity intersect with trauma and criminal behavior. For instance, Salo et al. (2022) conducted a study examining the relationship between adverse childhood experiences (ACEs), including developmental trauma, and later engagement in antisocial behaviors across different racial and ethnic groups. The findings revealed variations in the effects of ACEs on offending behaviors, with certain racial and ethnic groups being more vulnerable to the adverse effects of trauma. The study underscores the importance of considering racial and ethnic differences when examining the relationship between developmental trauma and criminal involvement.

Race and ethnicity also intersect with societal factors, such as systemic racism and discrimination, which can exacerbate the impact of trauma and contribute to offending behaviors. Research has shown that individuals from racially marginalized communities, who may experience higher rates of developmental trauma, also face challenges related to poverty, limited access to resources, and discrimination (Zhang & Monnat, 2021). These factors can contribute to a higher likelihood of engaging in criminal behavior as a coping mechanism or result of environmental factors.

2.4.2 Socio-economic Factors

Socio-economic factors, such as poverty and socio-economic status (SES), play a crucial role in understanding the relationship between developmental trauma and offending behaviors. Research has consistently demonstrated a link between SES and increased exposure to traumatic experiences, as well as higher rates of criminal involvement. Individuals from lower socio-economic backgrounds may face compounding challenges in addition to developmental trauma, including limited educational opportunities, inadequate healthcare, and limited access to social support (Trickett et al., 2011). These factors can contribute to a higher risk of engaging in antisocial or criminal behaviors as individuals may lack the necessary resources and support needed to cope effectively. Furthermore, individuals from lower SES backgrounds may experience increased exposure to community and neighborhood factors that can contribute to developmental trauma and criminal involvement. High-crime neighborhoods, limited access to positive role models, and prevalence of substance abuse may heighten the likelihood of engaging in criminal behavior as a response to adverse circumstances (Evans, 2004).

2.4.3 Implications and Considerations

Understanding the influence of race, ethnicity, and socio-economic factors on the relationship between developmental trauma and offending behaviors is crucial for addressing and implementing effective interventions. It is essential to consider the unique experiences and challenges faced by individuals from diverse racial and ethnic backgrounds as well as those from lower socio-economic backgrounds. Interventions should adopt a culturally sensitive and trauma-informed approach, recognizing the impact of systemic factors such as racism, discrimination, and poverty on individuals' experiences and behavior. Tailored interventions should aim to provide support, resources, and opportunities for healing and resilience specific to the needs and experiences of marginalized communities. The research reviewed indicates the disparities and challenges faced by individuals from marginalized communities and lower socio-economic backgrounds. By recognizing these factors and implementing culturally sensitive interventions, we can strive for greater equity and positive outcomes for those affected by developmental trauma and at risk of engaging in criminal behavior.

2.4.4 Case Analysis: The Case of John

In this case analysis, we will explore how race, ethnicity, and socio-economic factors influence the relationship between developmental trauma and offending behaviors. By examining a hypothetical case study, we can gain insights into the complex interplay between these factors and their impact on an individual's engagement in criminal behavior. This analysis aims to shed light on the unique experiences and challenges faced by individuals from diverse backgrounds, emphasizing the need for culturally sensitive interventions. Throughout the analysis, we will consider the potential effects of race, ethnicity, and socio-economic factors on individuals' trajectories.

The Case of John

John is a 19-year-old African American male living in a low-income neighborhood characterized by high crime rates, limited access to resources, and inadequate educational opportunities. He experienced significant developmental trauma during his childhood, witnessing domestic violence at home and being exposed to violence in his community. John also faced economic hardship and was frequently exposed to substance abuse within his environment.

Influences of Race and Ethnicity

As an African American, John may face unique challenges and experiences related to race and ethnicity. Systemic racism and discrimination can contribute to a higher likelihood of exposure to developmental trauma and limited opportunities for socio-economic advancement (Williams & Collins, 2016). The effects of historical and ongoing racism may affect John's perception of self, sense of belonging, and social integration, potentially influencing his engagement in criminal behavior as a coping mechanism or response to societal inequalities (Hinton et al., 2018).

Socio-Economic Factors and Developmental Trauma

Growing up in a low-income neighborhood and experiencing economic hardship put John at a disadvantage in terms of accessing resources and support. The lack of educational opportunities and exposure to substance abuse within his environment may have increased his vulnerability to developmental trauma (Evans, 2004). The interplay between socio-economic factors and trauma can contribute to the development of maladaptive coping strategies, which often manifest in engagement in offending behaviors. Limited access to positive role models, social support networks, and mental health services may further exacerbate the impact of developmental trauma on John's involvement in criminal activities (Zhang & Monnat, 2021).

Potential Interventions and Considerations

To address the relationship between developmental trauma, race, ethnicity, socio-economic factors, and offending behaviors, interventions should be sensitive to John's unique experiences and needs. Culturally competent approaches that acknowledge and address systemic racism, discrimination, and socio-economic inequities are crucial.

Community-based organizations can play a vital role in providing support and resources for individuals like John, offering mentoring, educational programs, and trauma-informed interventions tailored to racial and socio-economic contexts. Strengthening community connections and providing alternative pathways for John, such as vocational training or job placement programs, can help mitigate the risk factors associated with his socio-economic status.

Addressing systemic issues and promoting social justice is also essential. Advocacy efforts should focus on improving access to quality education, affordable housing, and healthcare services in marginalized communities. This involves addressing the root causes of inequality, dismantling systemic barriers, and fostering inclusive policies that support individuals affected by developmental trauma.

Conclusion

The case of John exemplifies the complex relationship between race, ethnicity, socio-economic factors, developmental trauma, and offending behaviors. By recognizing the unique challenges faced by individuals from diverse backgrounds, interventions can be developed to address the distinctive needs of marginalized communities. Culturally sensitive and trauma-informed approaches that consider the influence of race, ethnicity, and socio-economic factors can aid in promoting healing, resilience, and social reintegration while working towards addressing systemic inequities.

2.5 Conclusion

This chapter has provided an in-depth examination of the prevalence and characteristics of developmental trauma among offending populations. Studies consistently demonstrate higher rates of developmental trauma within offender populations compared to the general population. The long-term effects of developmental trauma on cognitive, emotional, and social functions are significant and contribute to the development of criminal behavior. Adverse childhood experiences, including abuse, neglect, and household dysfunction, are closely linked to the occurrence of developmental trauma among offenders. Finally, it is essential to consider the influence of race, ethnicity, and socio-economic factors on the relationship between trauma and offending, addressing the systemic barriers that exist. By understanding these factors, practitioners and policymakers can develop interventions and strategies that promote healing, resilience, and prevent further involvement in the criminal justice system.

References

Anda, R. F., Felitti, V. J., Bremner, J. D., Walker, J. D., Whitfield, C. L., Perry, B. D., Dube, S. R., & Giles, W. H. (2006). The enduring effects of abuse and related adverse experiences in childhood: A convergence of evidence from neurobiology and epidemiology. *European Archives of Psychiatry and Clinical Neuroscience, 256*(3), 174–186.

Briere, J., & Elliott, D. (2003). Prevalence and psychological sequelae of self-reported childhood physical and sexual abuse in a general population sample of men and women. *Child Abuse & Neglect, 27*(10), 1205–1222.

Coid, J., Petruckevitch, A., Chung, W. S., Richardson, J., Moorey, S., & Feder, G. (2013). Abusive experiences and psychiatric morbidity in women primary care attenders. *British Journal of Psychiatry, 183*(4), 332–339.

Dierkhising, C. B., Ko, S. J., Woods-Jaeger, B., Briggs, E. C., Lee, R., & Pynoos, R. S. (2013). Trauma histories among justice-involved youth: findings from the National Child Traumatic Stress Network. *European Journal of Psychotraumatology, 4*. https://doi.org/10.3402/ejpt.v4i0.20274

Dong, M., Anda, R. F., Felitti, V. J., Williamson, D. F., Dube, S. R., Brown, D. W., & Giles, W. H. (2005). Childhood residential mobility and multiple health risks during adolescence and adulthood: the hidden role of adverse childhood experiences. *Archives of Pediatrics & Adolescent Medicine, 159*(12), 1104–1110.

Evans, G. W. (2004). The environment of childhood poverty. *American Psychologist, 59*(2), 77–92.

Fazel, S., Doll, H., & Långström, N. (2008). Mental disorders among adolescents in juvenile detention and correctional facilities: A systematic review and metaregression analysis of 25 surveys. *Journal of the American Academy of Child & Adolescent Psychiatry, 47*(9), 1010–1019.

Felitti, V. J., Anda, R. F., Nordenberg, D., Williamson, D. F., Spitz, A. M., Edwards, V., Koss, M. P., & Marks, J. S. (1998). Relationship of childhood abuse and household dysfunction to many of the leading causes of death in adults: The Adverse Childhood Experiences (ACE) study. *American Journal of Preventive Medicine, 14*(4), 245–258.

Fergusson, D. M., Boden, J. M., & Horwood, L. J. (2008). Exposure to childhood sexual and physical abuse and adjustment in early adulthood. *Child Abuse & Neglect, 32*(6), 607–619.

Ford, J. D., Chapman, J., Mack, M., & Pearson, G. (2006). Pathways from traumatic child victimization to delinquency: Implications for juvenile and permanency court proceedings and decisions. *Juvenile and Family Court Journal, 57*(1), 13–26.

Ford, J. D., Grasso, D. J., Hawke, J., & Chapman, J. F. (2013). Poly-victimization among juvenile justice-involved youths. *Child Abuse & Neglect, 37*(10), 788–800.

Fox, B. H., Perez, N., Cass, E., Baglivio, M. T., & Epps, N. (2015). Trauma changes everything: Examining the relationship between adverse childhood experiences and serious, violent and chronic juvenile offenders. *Child Abuse & Neglect, 46*, 163–173.

Glaze, L. E., & Maruschak, L. M. (2010). Bureau of Justice Statistics. *US Dep't of Justice, Parents in Prison and Their Minor Children, at, 4*.

Herman, J. L. (2015). *Trauma and recovery*. Basic books.

Hinton, E., Henderson, L., & Reed, C. (2018). An unjust burden: The disparate treatment of Black Americans in the criminal justice system. *Vera Institute of Justice, 1*(1), 1–20.

Kendall-Tackett, K., Williams, L., & Finkelhor, D. (1993). Impact of sexual abuse on children: A review and synthesis of recent empirical studies. *Psychological Bulletin, 113*(1), 164–180.

Majer, M., Nater, U.M., Lin, JM.S. et al. Association of childhood trauma with cognitive function in healthy adults: a pilot study. BMC Neurology 10, 61 (2010). https://doi.org/10.1186/1471-2377-10-61.

Maniglio, R. (2015). Significance, nature, and direction of the association between child sexual abuse and conduct disorder: A systematic review. *Trauma, Violence, & Abuse, 16*(3), 241–257.

Merrick, M. T., Ports, K. A., Ford, D. C., Afifi, T. O., Gershoff, E. T., & Grogan-Kaylor, A. (2017). Unpacking the impact of adverse childhood experiences on adult mental health. *Child Abuse & Neglect, 69*, 10–19.

Repetti, R. L., Taylor, S. E., & Seeman, T. E. (2002). Risky families: Family social environments and the mental and physical health of offspring. *Psychological Bulletin, 128*(2), 330–366.

Salo, M., Appleton, A. A., & Tracy, M. (2022). Childhood adversity trajectories and violent behaviors in adolescence and early adulthood. *Journal of Interpersonal Violence, 37*(15–16), NP13978–NP14007. https://doi.org/10.1177/08862605211006366

Teicher, M. H., Andersen, S. L., Polcari, A., Anderson, C. M., & Navalta, C. P. (2002). Developmental neurobiology of childhood stress and trauma. *Psychiatric Clinics, 25*(2), 397–426.

Teicher, M. H., Samson, J. A., Polcari, A., & McGreenery, C. E. (2006). Sticks, stones, and hurtful words: relative effects of various forms of childhood maltreatment. *American Journal of Psychiatry, 163*(6), 993–1000.

Trickett, P. K., Negriff, S., Ji, J., & Peckins, M. (2011). Child maltreatment and adolescent development. *Journal of Research on Adolescence, 21*(1), 3–20.

Whitfield, C. L., Anda, R. F., Dube, S. R., & Felitti, V. J. (2003). Violent childhood experiences and the risk of intimate partner violence in adults: Assessment in a large health maintenance organization. *Journal of Interpersonal Violence, 18*(2), 166–185.

Williams, D. R., & Collins, C. (2016). *Racial residential segregation: A fundamental cause of racial disparities in health*. Public Health Reports.

Williams, M. T., Osman, M., Gran-Ruaz, S., & Lopez, J. (2021). Intersection of racism and PTSD: Assessment and treatment of racial stress and trauma. *Current Treatment Options in Psychiatry, 8*(4), 167–185.

Wrenn, G. L., Wingo, A. P., Moore, R., Pelletier, T., Gutman, A. R., Bradley, B., & Ressler, K. J. (2011). The effect of resilience on posttraumatic stress disorder in trauma-exposed inner-city primary care patients. *Journal of the National Medical Association, 103*(7), 560–566. https://doi.org/10.1016/s0027-9684(15)30381-3

Zhang, X., & Monnat, S. M. (2021). Racial/ethnic differences in clusters of adverse childhood experiences and associations with adolescent mental health. *SSM – Population Health, 17*, 100997. https://doi.org/10.1016/j.ssmph.2021.100997

Chapter 3
The Cycle of Developmental Trauma and Criminal Behavior

Developmental trauma refers to chronic or repetitive experiences of trauma during childhood that disrupt the normal course of development. Such experiences can range from physical or sexual abuse, neglect, witnessing violence, or prolonged exposure to stressors. The profound impact of such trauma extends far beyond its immediate effects, often leading to severe emotional, cognitive, and behavioral dysregulation, inevitably increasing the risk of involvement in criminal behavior later in life.

3.1 Theoretical Frameworks

Attachment theory provides a valuable framework to understand how early traumatic experiences can disrupt the formation of secure attachments, leading to insecure attachment patterns. These patterns, characterized by distrust, fear, and difficulty in forming healthy relationships, contribute to emotional dysregulation and impair an individual's ability to cope with distressing situations. Consequently, this maladaptive coping often leads to engagement in criminal behaviors as a means to satisfy unmet emotional needs or gain a sense of control and power.

Various psychological theories, including social learning theory, cognitive theory, and psychodynamic theory, elucidate the complex mechanisms underlying the association between developmental trauma and criminal behavior. Social learning theory posits that exposure to aggressive models and the reinforcement of violent behavior increases the likelihood of engaging in criminal acts. Cognitive theories focus on distorted thinking patterns and maladaptive belief systems that arise in response to trauma, leading to antisocial and criminal behavior. Additionally, psychodynamic theories explore how unresolved trauma manifests in unconscious drives, resulting in criminal acts as an outlet for repressed emotions and desires.

K. Sapp, *Exploring Developmental Trauma Disorder Among Offending Populations*, SpringerBriefs in Offending Populations & Correctional Psychotherapy,
https://doi.org/10.1007/978-3-031-61157-5_3

3.1.1 Attachment Theory

Attachment theory, proposed by John Bowlby, emphasizes the influential role of early attachment experiences on individuals' social and emotional development throughout their lives. According to the theory, the quality of early attachments serves as a blueprint for patterns of relating to others. Secure attachments, characterized by consistent, sensitive, and responsive caregiving, provide a secure base from which individuals feel safe to explore the world (Bowlby, 1988). Research has shown that individuals with secure attachments tend to display higher levels of resiliency, emotional regulation, and positive social interactions across the lifespan (Grossmann & Grossmann, 2006). In contrast, insecure attachments, characterized by inconsistent or unresponsive caregiving, can lead to difficulties in forming and maintaining relationships, emotional dysregulation, and increased vulnerability to psychopathology (Schore, 2001; Ainsworth et al., 2015). Understanding the impact of early attachments on individuals' developmental trajectories is critical for designing interventions and promoting healthy relationship experiences throughout life.

3.1.1.1 Attachment Disruption and Traumatic Experiences

Attachment disruption resulting from traumatic experiences and the absence of secure attachment relationships have been found to be associated with an increased risk of developing criminal behavior. Secure attachments play a crucial role in promoting positive social and emotional development, as they provide a foundation of trust, emotional support, and a sense of belonging (Bowlby, 1988). However, when individuals experience trauma, such as abuse, neglect, or loss, their ability to form and maintain secure attachments may be significantly compromised (Smith & Thornberry, 1995).

The absence of secure attachments can contribute to a range of negative outcomes, including an increased likelihood of engaging in criminal behavior. Individuals who lack secure attachments may struggle with emotional regulation, impulse control, and developing healthy relationships (Cullen, 1994). This can lead to maladaptive coping strategies, such as substance abuse, aggression, or delinquency, as a means to compensate for the unmet emotional needs and seek a sense of belonging and security (Wright et al., 2004). Additionally, the lack of secure attachments may impair individuals' ability to form positive social bonds, paving the way for involvement in criminal networks and deviant peer relationships (Laub & Sampson, 2003).

3.1.1.2 Insecure Attachment Patterns

When secure attachments are disrupted by traumatic experiences, children may develop insecure attachment patterns, including avoidant, anxious/ambivalent, or disorganized attachment styles. Avoidant attachment is characterized by the suppression of emotional needs and a tendency to avoid seeking comfort or support from others. Individuals with an avoidant attachment style may exhibit emotional distance in relationships as a strategy to protect themselves from rejection or disappointment (Ainsworth et al., 2015). Anxious/ambivalent attachment is marked by clinginess, anxiety, and ambivalence towards relationships. Individuals with this attachment style often exhibit heightened emotional reactions and a preoccupation with seeking reassurance due to inconsistent or unpredictable caregiving experiences (Ainsworth et al., 2015). Disorganized attachment represents a more complex and disoriented pattern. Individuals with disorganized attachment may display contradictory behaviors and appear frightened or disoriented in their interactions with caregivers. This attachment style often arises in the context of severe or disorganized trauma and can involve dissociative behaviors or a lack of clear strategies for managing attachment needs (Main & Solomon, 1990). Ultimately, these attachment patterns are characterized by difficulties in seeking and receiving support from others, emotional dysregulation, and challenges in forming trusting relationships (Main & Solomon, 1990).

3.1.1.2.1 Avoidant Attachment

Children who experience early developmental trauma, such as neglect, abandonment, or repeated disruptions in caregiving, are at a heightened risk of developing avoidant attachment patterns (Bowlby, 1988). These attachment patterns are often a product of adaptive coping strategies utilized by these children to protect themselves from further disappointment and emotional pain (Ainsworth et al., 2015).

Avoidant attachment can perpetuate a cycle of developmental trauma. Due to their emotional distancing and avoidance of seeking support, individuals with avoidant attachment patterns may struggle to establish secure and nurturing relationships later in life. This can lead to further experiences of rejection and isolation, reinforcing the underlying trauma. In turn, these recurring traumatic experiences may fuel the development of maladaptive behaviors, including criminal behavior, as individuals seek alternative means of coping and fulfillment.

Multiple studies have identified a potential association between avoidant attachment and the development of criminal behavior. Research by Moran et al. (2004) found that adolescents with avoidant attachment styles were more likely to engage in delinquent behaviors, including theft and substance abuse. Similarly, a study by Reijntjes et al. (2010) showed that avoidant attachment was associated with a higher risk of aggressive behavior in children and adolescents. These findings support the notion that avoidant attachment patterns contribute to the development of criminal behaviors. Furthermore, research by Main and Hesse (1990) revealed that individuals with disorganized attachment, which often includes avoidant features, were more likely to exhibit externalizing behaviors, including aggression, rule-breaking, and criminal activities. The disorganized attachment category represents a more severe form of insecure attachment linked to adverse childhood experiences, trauma, and disrupted caregiving.

Ultimately, avoidant attachment, stemming from experiences of developmental trauma, can significantly impact individuals' social and emotional development. The emotional distance and avoidance characterizing avoidant attachment patterns contribute to a perpetuating cycle of trauma, making individuals vulnerable to the development of maladaptive behaviors, including criminal behavior. Understanding the link between avoidant attachment and the development of criminal behavior is crucial for implementing interventions that promote secure attachment relationships, address underlying trauma, and provide appropriate support for individuals at risk. By breaking the cycle of developmental trauma, promoting healthy coping strategies, and fostering resilience, it is possible to mitigate the likelihood of individuals engaging in criminal behavior and facilitate positive pathways of growth and recovery.

3.1.1.2.2 Anxious/Ambivalent Attachment

Children who experience early developmental trauma, such as inconsistent or unpredictable caregiving or maltreatment, are at an increased risk of developing anxious/ambivalent attachment patterns (Ainsworth et al., 2015). These attachment patterns often emerge as adaptive coping mechanisms, as children attempt to navigate the ambiguity and unpredictability of their caregiving environment. Anxious/ambivalent attachment can perpetuate a cycle of developmental trauma. Children with anxious/ambivalent attachment patterns often experience heightened emotional reactions, anxiety, and a need for constant reassurance due to inconsistent or unavailable caregiving (Ainsworth et al., 2015). Consequently, these children may struggle to form secure and stable relationships, leading to repeated experiences of rejection, disappointment, and abandonment. These recurring traumatic experiences reinforce the anxious/ambivalent attachment pattern, potentially leading to the development of maladaptive behaviors, such as criminal behaviors, to cope with unresolved emotional distress.

Several studies have identified a potential association between anxious/ambivalent attachment and the development of criminal behaviors. Research by Kočovská et al. (2012) found that adolescents with anxious/ambivalent attachment patterns were more likely to exhibit aggressive and delinquent behaviors. These individuals may resort to acts of aggression or delinquency as a way to cope with their underlying emotional turmoil and to gain a sense of control or attention in their interpersonal interactions.

Moreover, research by Moffitt and Caspi (2001) demonstrated that individuals with persistent anxious/ambivalent attachment patterns were more likely to engage in criminal activities later in life. The study utilized data from the Dunedin Multidisciplinary Health and Development Study, a longitudinal study that followed a cohort of individuals from birth into adulthood. The researchers assessed the participants' attachment patterns using behavioral observations, interviews, and questionnaires at various stages of their development. The findings of the study revealed that individuals with persistently high levels of anxious/ambivalent attachment throughout childhood and adolescence were more likely to engage in criminal behaviors later in life. These behaviors included acts of violence, property offenses, and persistent antisocial conduct. The association between anxious/ambivalent attachment and criminal behaviors persisted even after taking into account other pertinent factors such as socio-economic status, family background, and previous conduct problems. The researchers proposed that individuals with persistent anxious/ambivalent attachment patterns face unique challenges in emotion regulation, impulse control, and the formation of stable relationships. The chronic instability and unpredictability experienced by these individuals within their attachment relationships may contribute to a heightened vulnerability for engaging in criminal behaviors as a coping mechanism or a means to gain attention and control in their interactions.

The research by Moffitt and Caspi (2001) provided valuable insights into the long-term consequences of anxious/ambivalent attachment and its association with criminal behaviors. It highlighted the importance of early interventions that address attachment-related issues and provide support to individuals at risk, aiming to foster healthy socioemotional development and prevent the onset of criminal behaviors. The chronic instability and uncertainties associated with anxious/ambivalent attachment can hinder emotional regulation, impulse control, and the development of healthy relationships, contributing to a vulnerability for criminal behaviors.

In conclusion, anxious/ambivalent attachment, resulting from experiences of developmental trauma, can significantly impact individuals' socioemotional development and increase the risk of engaging in criminal behaviors. The cycle of developmental trauma perpetuated by anxious/ambivalent attachment involves an interplay between unresolved emotional distress, repeated experiences of disappointment or rejection, and the development of maladaptive coping strategies, potentially leading to criminal behaviors. Understanding the relationship between anxious/ambivalent attachment and the development of criminal behaviors is essential for implementing interventions aimed at promoting secure attachment, providing trauma-informed care, and offering appropriate support for individuals at risk. By breaking the cycle of developmental trauma, promoting resilience, and fostering healthy coping strategies, it is possible to mitigate the likelihood of individuals engaging in criminal behaviors and fostering positive pathways of growth and recovery.

3.1.1.2.3 Disorganized Attachment

Children who experience early developmental trauma, such as maltreatment, abuse, or caregiver disruptions, are at an increased risk of developing disorganized attachment patterns (Bowlby, 1988). In disorganized attachment, children face conflicting and frightening caregiving experiences that lead to confusion and disorientation in their attachment behaviors. The disruption in attachment relationships resulting from disorganized attachment creates an adverse environment, amplifying the risk of experiencing further traumatic events (Crittenden & Spieker, 2018). The cycle continues as individuals with disorganized attachment patterns struggle to establish stable and supportive relationships, increasing the likelihood of engaging in maladaptive coping strategies, such as criminal behaviors, to manage unresolved stress and trauma.

Extensive research has established a compelling association between disorganized attachment and the development of criminal behaviors. Lyons-Ruth and Jacobvitz (2008) conducted a comprehensive review and analysis of existing research on disorganized attachment and its association with behavioral and psychological difficulties. They reviewed a wide range of studies involving both clinical and non-clinical samples to understand the implications of disorganized attachment across different developmental stages. Their findings highlighted several key associations between disorganized attachment and negative outcomes. Some of the behavioral and psychological problems linked to disorganized attachment include:

1. Aggression and Externalizing Behaviors:
   Children with a history of disorganized attachment have been found to exhibit higher levels of aggression, conduct problems, and externalizing behaviors compared to children with other attachment classifications. These behaviors often persist into adolescence and early adulthood.
2. Internalizing Problems:
   Disorganized attachment has also been associated with internalizing problems such as anxiety, depression, and withdrawal. These internalizing difficulties may manifest in various ways throughout the lifespan.
3. Social and Relational Difficulties:
   Individuals with a history of disorganized attachment may struggle with forming and maintaining relationships, experiencing difficulties with trust, intimacy, and emotional regulation. These challenges can persist into adulthood and affect various social and interpersonal domains.
4. Trauma and Post-Traumatic Stress Disorder (PTSD):
   Disorganized attachment has been found to increase the risk of exposure to traumatic experiences in childhood. This, in turn, can contribute to the development of post-traumatic stress symptoms and disorders later in life.
5. Emotion Regulation and Dysregulation:
   Disorganized attachment has been associated with difficulties in emotion regulation. Individuals with disorganized attachment may have challenges in

managing and expressing their emotions in adaptive ways, leading to emotional dysregulation and impulsivity.

It's important to note that while disorganized attachment is associated with an increased risk for these behavioral and psychological problems, it does not imply that all individuals with disorganized attachment will develop these difficulties. Other factors such as genetic predisposition, environmental influences, and protective factors also play a significant role in shaping outcomes. Overall, the study by Lyons-Ruth and Jacobvitz (2008) underscores the importance of recognizing the impact of disorganized attachment on various aspects of psychological well-being and functioning.

Longitudinal studies indicate that individuals with a history of disorganized attachment can also face persistent challenges in adulthood (Lyons-Ruth et al., 2016). These studies have highlighted the long-term consequences and implications of disorganized attachment for psychological well-being and functioning. Here are two notable longitudinal studies that support this claim:

1. The Minnesota Longitudinal Study (Main et al., 1985):
   This study followed a sample of 101 participants from infancy to early adulthood, examining the developmental outcomes associated with different attachment patterns. Individuals with a history of disorganized attachment were found to be at an increased risk for a range of negative outcomes. In adulthood, individuals with disorganized attachment histories exhibited higher rates of psychological distress, difficulties in relationships, and greater vulnerability to mental health issues, such as depression and anxiety (Main et al., 1985).
2. The Berkeley Guidance Study (Lyons-Ruth et al., 1993):
   This longitudinal study followed a sample of individuals from infancy to adulthood to examine the links between early attachment patterns and outcomes in later life. The findings showed that individuals with a history of disorganized attachment experienced challenges in various domains of functioning, including emotional regulation, interpersonal relationships, and overall psychological well-being. Disorganized attachment was associated with an increased risk for psychopathology, such as borderline personality disorder and dissociative symptoms, as well as difficulties in establishing and maintaining stable intimate relationships (Lyons-Ruth et al., 1993).

These studies, along with other longitudinal research, provide robust evidence supporting the long-term impact of disorganized attachment on adult functioning. The findings suggest that disorganized attachment patterns disrupt the development of adaptive strategies for managing stress, regulating emotions, and forming secure relationships. Consequently, individuals with a history of disorganized attachment may face ongoing challenges in their psychological, social, and relational well-being throughout adulthood.

Understanding these associations can inform intervention and support strategies aimed at promoting healthy development and addressing the specific needs of individuals with disorganized attachment histories. The disorganized attachment pattern disrupts the development of self-regulation and emotional stability, predisposing individuals to impulsivity and impaired decision-making (Crittenden & Spieker, 2018). These deficits contribute to a heightened vulnerability for engaging in criminal acts, such as aggression, violent offenses, and substance abuse, as individuals seek alternative ways to cope with internal distress and regulate their emotions (Main & Hesse, 1990). Moreover, disorganized attachment has been implicated in the formation of deviant peer relationships and associations with criminal networks, further perpetuating a cycle of criminal behavior (Laub & Sampson, 2003).

3.1.1.2.4 Case Analysis: Insecure Attachment Styles, Developmental Trauma, and Criminal Behavior

This case analysis focuses on the relationship between insecure attachment styles, the cycle of developmental trauma, and its potential impact on criminal behavior. The case study explores the experiences of John, a fictional individual who exhibits an anxious-ambivalent attachment style and has a history of developmental trauma. Through an analysis of John's attachment patterns, trauma experiences, and subsequent involvement in criminal behavior, the study highlights the potential connections between insecure attachment, trauma, and criminal outcomes.

Case Analysis of John's Attachment Patterns, Trauma Experience, and Involvement of Criminal Behavior

John is a 19-year-old individual who exhibits an anxious-ambivalent attachment style. His childhood was characterized by inconsistent care, emotional neglect, and witnessing domestic violence. These adverse experiences contributed to John's insecure attachment, impacting his emotional regulation, interpersonal relationships, and overall development. This case analysis aims to explore the potential influences of John's insecure attachment style, the cycle of developmental trauma, and their impact on his involvement in criminal behavior.

Attachment Patterns:

John's anxious-ambivalent attachment style is rooted in his early childhood experiences. He demonstrates an intense fear of abandonment, constant need for reassurance, and an inclination to over-analyze relationships. These attachment patterns stem from his inconsistent caregiving experiences, which influenced his perception of relationships as unpredictable and unreliable. Consequently, John struggles to establish healthy and secure connections with others, hindering his ability to form stable relationships and seek support when facing adversities.

Developmental Trauma:

John's upbringing was marked by various developmental traumas. He experienced emotional neglect, as his parents were often emotionally absent and failed to provide consistent nurturing. Additionally, he witnessed frequent domestic violence between his parents, which exposed him to chronic fear and disrupted his sense of safety. These traumatic experiences compromised his emotional regulation, cognitive development, and social skills, exacerbating his attachment-related insecurities.

Impact on Emotional Regulation:

John's insecure attachment style and developmental trauma have significantly impacted his emotional regulation abilities. He struggles to manage and express his emotions effectively, often experiencing intense feelings of anxiety, anger, and fear of rejection. The inability to regulate these emotions leaves him vulnerable to impulsive behaviors, difficulty coping with stressors, and a heightened need for immediate gratification or escape mechanisms.

Criminal Behavior:

Given his attachment-related insecurities, unresolved developmental trauma, and impaired emotional regulation, John has become involved in criminal behavior. Seeking validation and a sense of power, he has resorted to engaging in illicit activities such as theft and substance abuse. These behaviors temporarily alleviate his emotional distress and provide an illusion of control, but they perpetuate a cycle of self-destructive patterns and increase his risk of further involvement in criminal behavior.

Cyclical Nature:

John's involvement in criminal behavior further perpetuates the cycle of developmental trauma and reinforces his insecure attachment style. Engaging in criminal activities exposes him to risky situations, potential revictimization, and further disruption of healthy relationships. These experiences exacerbate his emotional dysregulation and perpetuate the belief that interpersonal connections are unreliable and potentially harmful, reinforcing his need for immediate gratification and maladaptive coping strategies.

This case analysis highlights the interconnectedness between insecure attachment styles, the cycle of developmental trauma, and its potential influence on criminal behavior. John's anxious-ambivalent attachment style, rooted in inconsistent caregiving and witnessing domestic violence, exacerbates his developmental trauma experiences. The resulting impaired emotional regulation, coupled with a desire for validation and control, contribute to his involvement in criminal activities. This case emphasizes the importance of early intervention, recognizing and addressing attachment-related challenges, and providing therapeutic support to break the cycle of insecure attachment, trauma, and subsequent criminal behavior.

3.1.1.3 Conclusion

Attachment theory provides insight into how traumatic experiences can disrupt the formation of secure attachments during early childhood. Insecure attachment patterns can develop as a result, significantly impacting individuals' social and emotional functioning throughout their lives. Understanding this disruption is crucial for developing effective interventions, trauma-informed care, and targeted therapies aimed at promoting healing and the development of secure attachments for those who have experienced trauma.

3.1.2 Psychological Theories

Various psychological theories, including social learning theory, cognitive theory, and psychodynamic theory, elucidate the complex mechanisms underlying the association between developmental trauma and criminal behavior. Social learning theory posits that exposure to aggressive models and the reinforcement of violent behavior increases the likelihood of engaging in criminal acts. Cognitive theories focus on distorted thinking patterns and maladaptive belief systems that arise in response to trauma, leading to antisocial and criminal behavior. Additionally, psychodynamic theories explore how unresolved trauma manifests in unconscious drives, resulting in criminal acts as an outlet for repressed emotions and desires.

3.1.2.1 Social Learning Theory

The social learning theory proposes that individuals learn behavior through observation, imitation, and reinforcement. In the context of criminal behavior, this theory further suggests that exposure to developmental trauma can play a significant role. As such, social learning theory provides a framework for understanding the association between developmental trauma and criminal behavior. Individuals exposed to trauma may observe and imitate antisocial behavior as means of coping or survival (Bandura, 1973). They may learn violence as a means of attaining power or control, especially if they witnessed and experienced violence during their early development. Empirical studies have provided substantial evidence of this association.

3.1.2.1.1 Impact of Childhood Abuse and Neglect on Criminal Behavior: A Study by Widom (1989)

Widom (1989) conducted a groundbreaking study that examined the relationship between childhood abuse/neglect, social learning theory, and criminal behavior. Widom's study utilized a prospective cohort design, following individuals with documented cases of child abuse and neglect alongside a matched control group.

The study included a sample of 908 individuals, with over half having a history of abuse or neglect. The methodology involved data collection through extensive official records, including court documents, child protective services reports, and criminal justice records. The study aimed to investigate the relationship between childhood maltreatment and subsequent criminal behavior into adulthood.

Widom's study demonstrated a significant association between childhood abuse, neglect, and criminal behavior. The findings revealed that individuals who experienced childhood maltreatment were more likely to engage in criminal activities later in life compared to the control group. Specifically, abused, and neglected individuals were more prone to committing violent offenses, property crimes, and drug-related offenses. The study also revealed a higher risk of arrests and convictions among the maltreated group. These findings establish a clear link between childhood abuse, neglect, and an increased likelihood of criminal behavior.

The study conducted by Widom (1989) holds significant implications for both theoretical and practical realms. Firstly, the study supports and strengthens the foundations of social learning theory by demonstrating that exposure to early adverse experiences, such as child abuse and neglect, can contribute to the adoption of criminal behavior through observational learning and reinforcement processes. Moreover, Widom's findings underline the long-lasting effects of childhood maltreatment. The traumatic experiences endured during childhood disrupt social and emotional development, leading to maladaptive coping strategies and an increased vulnerability to engage in criminal behavior. Therefore, the study suggests that interventions focused on preventing and addressing childhood abuse and neglect could contribute to reducing the risk of criminal involvement. Furthermore, the study highlights the importance of early intervention and the implementation of effective support systems and programs for individuals who have experienced childhood maltreatment. Such interventions may help break the cycle of trauma and provide individuals with alternative strategies for coping with adversity, reducing the likelihood of engaging in criminal behavior.

Although Widom's study provided critical insights into the association between childhood abuse, neglect, and criminal behavior, it is essential to acknowledge its limitations. The sample predominantly consisted of individuals from low socioeconomic backgrounds, affecting the generalizability of the findings. Moreover, the study relied on official records, which might not capture the full extent of criminal behavior or provide a comprehensive understanding of the individuals' experiences. Further research is warranted to delve deeper into the mechanisms through which childhood abuse and neglect influence criminal behavior. Longitudinal studies incorporating qualitative interviews and a more diverse range of participants may provide a more comprehensive understanding of the complexities involved.

Overall, Widom's study (1989) served as a pivotal contribution to the understanding of the association between childhood abuse, neglect, and criminal behavior. The findings underscore the significance of social learning theory and emphasize the lasting impact of developmental trauma on an individual's propensity to engage in criminal activities. The implications of this study call for preventative measures, early intervention programs, and support systems to break the cycle of maltreatment and reduce the risk of future criminal involvement.

3.1.2.1.2 Childhood Traumatic Experiences and Delinquency: A Study by Loeber et al. (1998)

Loeber et al. (1998) study employed a longitudinal design to examine the association between mental health, including the influence of childhood traumatic experiences, and delinquency. The study utilized a large sample of 1517 participants comprising of 3 samples of boys, who were followed from childhood to adolescence and into adulthood. The study included a comprehensive assessment of childhood traumatic experiences and delinquent behaviors, including violent offenses, property crimes, and other forms of delinquency. Data collection involved various sources, including self-report measures, parental reports, official records, and collateral interviews.

The findings of Loeber et al. (1998) study demonstrated a significant relationship between mental health, to include childhood traumatic experiences and delinquent behavior. Participants who reported experiencing childhood trauma were more likely to engage in delinquent acts compared to those who did not report such experiences. The study revealed that childhood traumatic events, such as physical abuse, sexual abuse, or witnessing violence, significantly increased the risk of later delinquency. Additionally, the study found that the effects of traumatic experiences persisted into adolescence and adulthood, suggesting a long-lasting impact.

Loeber et al. (1998) study provides important implications for understanding the link between childhood trauma and delinquency. The findings support the notion that traumatic experiences during childhood can disrupt normal development processes, leading to an increased risk of engaging in delinquent behaviors. The study highlights the role of social learning mechanisms in this association, suggesting that exposure to violence and trauma within the family environment can influence the adoption of deviant behaviors through observational learning and reinforcement processes. Furthermore, the study emphasizes the need for early identification and intervention programs targeting individuals who have experienced childhood trauma. Recognizing the impact of traumatic experiences on delinquency can aid in the development of appropriate prevention strategies and therapeutic interventions. By addressing the underlying trauma and providing support, individuals may develop healthier coping mechanisms, reducing the likelihood of engaging in delinquent acts.

One limitation of Loeber et al. (1998) study is the reliance on self-report measures, which may introduce bias and underreporting of traumatic experiences or delinquent behaviors. Additionally, the study mainly focused on quantitative data, limiting the exploration of subjective experiences and contextual factors that may influence the association between childhood trauma and delinquency. Future research should utilize mixed methods approaches, incorporating qualitative techniques to understand the lived experiences and underlying mechanisms better.

Longitudinal studies encompassing a broader range of sociodemographic factors and incorporating diverse populations would enhance our knowledge in this field.

In conclusion, Loeber et al. (1998) shed light on the association between childhood traumatic experiences, mental health, and delinquent behavior. The findings underscore the lasting impact of such experiences on an individual's propensity to engage in delinquency, highlighting the role of social learning processes. The study's implications call for early intervention programs and therapeutic interventions that address childhood trauma to prevent delinquent behaviors and promote healthier developmental outcomes.

3.1.2.1.3 Longitudinal Study of Risk Factors for Delinquency: Thornberry et al. (2001)

Thornberry et al. (2001) conducted a study focusing on the association between adverse childhood experiences, social learning processes, and violent offending. The research followed a sample of 1354 participants over a long period, starting in adolescence and extending into adulthood. Furthermore, the study employed various data sources, including self-report surveys, official records, and information from parents, teachers, and community members. By collecting data across multiple domains, the study aimed to identify the interplay of risk factors and their impact on delinquency.

Thornberry et al. (2001) study yielded several significant findings regarding the risk factors for delinquency. The study identified various individual and contextual factors that significantly contributed to the likelihood of engaging in delinquent behaviors. These risk factors included family dynamics, antisocial peers, substance abuse, school experiences, and neighborhood characteristics. The study found that individuals exposed to multiple risk factors exhibited higher delinquency rates than those with fewer risk factors. Furthermore, the study also identified protective factors, such as positive parental involvement, meaningful educational experiences, and prosocial peers, which served to mitigate the risk of engaging in delinquent behaviors. Moreover, the findings revealed that risk factors in early adolescence had a cumulative effect, influencing delinquency throughout the life course.

Thornberry et al. (2001) study has significant implications for understanding the etiology of delinquency and the development of effective prevention and intervention strategies. The findings emphasize the importance of targeting multiple levels of influence, including individual, family, peer, school, and neighborhood factors. Comprehensive approaches that address these contexts can help reduce the risk of delinquency by enhancing protective factors and minimizing risk factors. The study underscores the need for early identification and intervention programs that target individuals at risk of delinquency. By addressing risk factors in early adolescence, interventions can potentially interrupt developmental pathways and promote positive outcomes. Additionally, the study highlights the crucial role of supportive family environments, positive educational experiences, and healthy peer relationships in promoting prosocial behaviors and reducing delinquent tendencies.

One limitation of Thornberry et al. (2001) study is the reliance on self-report measures, which may introduce social desirability bias and underreporting of delinquent behaviors. Additionally, the study relied on a predominantly urban sample, limiting the generalizability of the findings to other populations and contexts. Future research should consider incorporating more diverse samples to allow for a better understanding of the different risk factors that may emerge across various settings. Longitudinal studies that extend into adulthood can provide insights into the long-term effects of early risk factors on delinquency and subsequent adult outcomes.

In conclusion, Thornberry et al. (2001) study provides valuable insights into the risk factors associated with delinquent behaviors. The findings highlight the complexity of delinquency etiology, emphasizing the importance of multifaceted approaches in prevention and intervention efforts. By addressing risk factors and promoting protective factors, interventions can help reduce the occurrence of delinquency and enhance positive developmental trajectories.

3.1.2.2 Cognitive Theories

Cognitive theories, such as social cognitive theory and cognitive behavioral theory, are widely used in understanding criminal behavior. These theories emphasize the role of cognitive processes, including thoughts, beliefs, and attitudes, in shaping individuals' behaviors. According to social cognitive theory, individuals learn through observation, modeling, and reinforcement. Cognitive behavioral theory focuses on how cognitive processes, such as cognitive distortions and faulty thinking patterns, influence behavior.

Several cognitive processes contribute to the cycle of developmental trauma and criminal behavior. Firstly, individuals who experience trauma may develop maladaptive cognitive schemas, such as a negative self-image or a distrust of others. These cognitive schemas can lead to distorted thinking patterns and contribute to pro-criminal attitudes and beliefs. For example, a person may develop a belief that aggression is an acceptable way to solve problems due to their exposure to violence.

Secondly, cognitive biases, such as attentional biases and memory biases, play a role in the cycle of trauma and criminal behavior. Attentional biases can lead individuals to focus more on aggressive or threatening environmental cues. Memory biases can result in the overemphasis and exaggeration of previous violent or traumatic experiences. These biases reinforce the cycle of trauma and increase the likelihood of engaging in criminal behavior.

Thirdly, cognitive deficits, such as difficulties with impulse control, decision-making, and problem-solving, are common in individuals who have experienced developmental trauma. These deficits may lead to impulsive and rash decision-making, heightened aggression, and difficulty finding adaptive solutions to conflicts, contributing to a higher risk of criminal behavior.

Understanding the association between cognitive theories, developmental trauma, and criminal behavior is crucial for developing effective interventions. Therapeutic interventions can aim to address and modify maladaptive cognitive schemas, correct cognitive biases, and improve cognitive functioning. Cognitive-behavioral therapy (CBT) is commonly used to challenge distorted thinking patterns, develop cognitive skills, and reduce criminal behavior risk. In addition to individual-focused interventions, it is essential to address the environmental factors that perpetuate the cycle of trauma and criminal behavior. This includes providing trauma-informed care, creating supportive and safe communities, and offering opportunities for positive social learning experiences. Implementing preventive interventions that address cognitive deficits, such as programs focusing on impulse control and problem-solving skills training, can also be beneficial.

In conclusion, the association between cognitive theories, developmental trauma, and criminal behavior highlights the complex interplay of cognitive processes in shaping individuals' behaviors. This knowledge provides insights into the development and perpetuation of criminal behavior, emphasizing the importance of addressing cognitive factors in interventions aimed at breaking the cycle of trauma and reducing criminal recidivism.

3.1.2.3 Psychodynamic Theories

Psychodynamic theories, such as psychoanalysis and attachment theory, offer insights into the psychological processes that contribute to criminal behavior (Freud, 1961; Bowlby, 1969). These theories emphasize unconscious drives, early-life experiences, and the impact of relationships on individual development. Psychodynamic perspectives emphasize the role of unresolved conflicts, defense mechanisms, and maladaptive psychosocial development in shaping personality traits and behaviors.

Several psychodynamic processes contribute to the cycle of developmental trauma and criminal behavior. Firstly, unresolved conflicts and unmet needs from early-life experiences can manifest as maladaptive coping strategies, impulsivity, and aggression (Fonagy et al., 2018). Individuals may engage in criminal behavior as a way to cope with their unresolved emotional pain or to gain a sense of control in their chaotic lives.

Secondly, defense mechanisms, such as repression, denial, or displacement, can play a role in the cycle of trauma and criminal behavior. These defense mechanisms serve to protect individuals from painful memories and emotions associated with their traumatic experiences. However, they can also lead to distorted perceptions of reality, difficulty taking responsibility for one's actions, and an external locus of control, all of which can contribute to criminal behavior (Freud, 1961).

Thirdly, attachment disruptions and insecure attachment patterns resulting from developmental trauma influence individuals' ability to establish healthy relationships and regulate emotions effectively (Bowlby, 1969). Lack of secure attachments can contribute to difficulties in developing empathy, forming healthy social connections, and adhering to societal norms, all of which are associated with an increased risk of engaging in criminal behavior (van Ijzendoorn et al., 1999).

Understanding the association between psychodynamic theories, developmental trauma, and criminal behavior has implications for intervention strategies. Psychodynamic interventions, such as psychodynamic therapy or trauma-focused therapy, can help individuals explore and resolve unconscious conflicts, process traumatic memories, and develop healthier coping mechanisms (Fonagy et al., 2018). These interventions aim to address underlying psychological issues that contribute to criminal behavior.

Moreover, interventions that focus on attachment repair and the development of secure relationships can help individuals form healthier social connections and enhance their ability to regulate emotions effectively. Trauma-informed care, which involves recognizing and addressing the impacts of trauma, can also be beneficial in creating a safe and supportive environment for individuals who have experienced developmental trauma. Community-based programs that provide support, education, and opportunities for skill-building can also be valuable in breaking the cycle of trauma and criminal behavior. These programs aim to address underlying psychosocial difficulties, improve coping skills, and reduce risk factors associated with criminal behavior.

Overall, the association between psychodynamic theories, developmental trauma, and criminal behavior illuminates the complex psychological processes involved in the development and perpetuation of criminal behavior. By acknowledging the impact of early-life experiences on psychosocial development, psychodynamic perspectives offer valuable insights into the underlying factors contributing to criminal behavior. These insights can inform interventions aimed at addressing unresolved conflicts, improving attachment patterns, and breaking the cycle of trauma and criminal behavior.

3.2 The Interplay of Developmental Trauma, Psychopathology, and Criminal Behavior

Developmental trauma can significantly increase the risk of developing psychopathology. The traumatic experiences disrupt normal developmental processes, leading to maladaptive social, cognitive and emotional functioning. Trauma affects the brain's stress response systems, contributing to the dysregulation of neurotransmitters and hormonal systems implicated in mental health disorders (Teicher et al., 2016). These biological alterations, combined with psychological factors, including negative self-perceptions, impaired social interactions, and emotional dysregulation, contribute to the manifestation of psychopathological symptoms (Gold et al., 2016) often leading to the development of psychopathological disorders, such as post-traumatic stress disorder (PTSD), depression, anxiety, or borderline personality (Spinazzola et al., 2014).

Psychopathology is strongly associated with an increased risk of engaging in criminal behavior. Certain mental health disorders, such as conduct disorder, antisocial personality disorder, or substance use disorders, are particularly linked to criminal involvement (Fazel et al., 2012). Individuals with these disorders may exhibit impulsivity, impaired judgment, aggression, and difficulties with inhibitory control, all of which increase the likelihood of engaging in criminal acts. Moreover, the self-medication hypothesis suggests that individuals with psychopathology may turn to substance abuse as a coping mechanism, further increasing their risk of criminal behavior (Otasowie, 2021).

Developmental trauma acts as a significant contributor to the development of psychopathology and subsequently influences the pathway to criminal behavior. Trauma can disrupt the normal trajectory of psychosocial development, impairing the acquisition of adaptive coping mechanisms, problem-solving skills, and prosocial behavior. These deficits, combined with the presence of psychopathological symptoms, create a fertile ground for engaging in criminal behavior as a means of coping with internal and environmental stressors (Briere et al., 2005).

Understanding the interplay between developmental trauma, psychopathology, and criminal behavior is essential for effective interventions and prevention strategies. Trauma-informed therapy approaches, such as trauma-focused cognitive-behavioral therapy (TF-CBT) or eye movement desensitization and reprocessing (EMDR), help individuals process their traumatic experiences, alleviate psychopathological symptoms, and reduce the risk of engaging in criminal behavior (Cohen et al., 2016). Integrated interventions that address both trauma and psychopathology yield the most favorable outcomes. Additionally, targeted prevention efforts should focus on creating supportive environments, promoting positive parenting practices, and identifying and addressing trauma early in life. Early detection and intervention for at-risk individuals can help mitigate the impact of trauma, reduce psychopathological symptoms, and prevent future criminal behavior.

In conclusion, the interplay between developmental trauma, psychopathology, and criminal behavior is complex and multifaceted. Developmental trauma can lead to the development of psychopathology, which, in turn, increases the risk of engaging in criminal behavior. Understanding these interconnections is vital for the development of effective interventions and prevention strategies that address both trauma and psychopathology, aiming to break the cycle of victimization, mental health difficulties, and criminal involvement.

3.2.1 *Case Analysis: The Interplay of Developmental Trauma, Psychopathology, and Criminal Behavior*

This case analysis examines the interplay between developmental trauma, psychopathology, and criminal behavior in the context of a specific individual's life. By exploring the complex dynamics between these factors, we gain insight into the reciprocal relationships and understand how they contribute to the individual's behavior. The analysis integrates theories and empirical evidence to provide a comprehensive understanding of the case.

Case of James
Case Background:

The case involves a 25-year-old individual, named James, who experienced severe developmental trauma during childhood. He was exposed to domestic violence, neglect, and physical abuse, which had a lasting impact on his emotional well-being and cognitive functioning. As James grew older, he developed symptoms of psychopathology, including post-traumatic stress disorder (PTSD), depression, and impulsivity. These symptoms, combined with limited social support, have substantially increased the risk of his involvement in criminal behavior.

Interplay of Developmental Trauma and Psychopathology:

The developmental trauma James experienced disrupted his normal developmental processes, leading to the development of psychopathological symptoms. Trauma can alter the brain's stress response systems, affecting neurotransmitters and hormonal regulation associated with mental health disorders (Teicher et al., 2016). James's PTSD symptoms emerged as a result of his traumatic experiences, impacting his cognitive appraisal of threat and his ability to regulate emotions effectively (Briere et al., 2005). The trauma also contributed to James's depression, creating negative self-perceptions and impairing his social interactions (Spinazzola et al., 2014).

Psychopathology and Criminal Behavior:

James's psychopathological symptoms play a crucial role in his engagement in criminal behavior. Impulsivity, a common feature of several psychopathological disorders, can lead individuals to act on immediate desires without considering the consequences (Hofmann et al., 2008). For James, impulsivity increases the likelihood of engaging in impulsive and potentially criminal acts, such as substance abuse, theft, or physical altercations. Depression, often associated with reduced inhibition and a negative view of oneself and the world, can also contribute to engagement in criminal behavior as a means of escape or self-medication (Gvion & Apter, 2012; Otasowie, 2021).

Impact on Treatment and Rehabilitation:

Understanding the interplay of developmental trauma, psychopathology, and criminal behavior is crucial for effective treatment and rehabilitation. In James's case, a comprehensive approach is needed to address the underlying trauma, psychopathological symptoms, and criminal conduct. Trauma-focused therapies, such as eye movement desensitization and reprocessing (EMDR) or cognitive-behavioral therapy (CBT), can help James process and heal from his traumatic experiences (Cohen et al., 2016). Addressing his psychopathological symptoms through medication, therapy, or a combination of both is important for symptom management and improving his emotional well-being. Additionally, incorporating cognitive-behavioral interventions to enhance impulse control and develop more adaptive coping strategies can aid in reducing James's engagement in criminal behavior (DeLisi et al., 2016).

Prevention and Support Strategies:

To prevent the intergenerational transmission of developmental trauma and criminal behavior, early intervention and support strategies must be implemented. Identifying and addressing trauma and psychopathological symptoms in childhood can mitigate their long-term effects and prevent future criminal involvement (DeCandia & Guarino, 2020). Implementing trauma-informed approaches in educational settings, social services, and the criminal justice system can help create supportive and healing environments that address the root causes of behavior (Covington, 2022; Ford et al., 2013).

The case analysis of James highlights the intricate interplay between developmental trauma, psychopathology, and criminal behavior. The traumatic experiences during James's childhood shaped his psychopathological symptoms, which, in turn, contributed to his engagement in criminal behavior. By recognizing and addressing the underlying trauma and psychopathology, tailored interventions can be implemented to break the cycle and facilitate James's rehabilitation and reintegration into society.

3.3 The Cycle of Developmental Trauma and Criminal Behavior

The cycle of developmental trauma and criminal behavior often unfolds in a cyclical pattern. Experiences of trauma during childhood frequently lead to disrupted social and academic functioning, alienation from prosocial peers, and educational setbacks. Furthermore, it leads to the internalization of negative self-image, impaired emotional regulation, and disrupted attachment styles (Perry, 2002). These adverse consequences substantially increase the likelihood of getting involved in delinquent behaviors, gang affiliation, and ultimately criminal offenses. Once engaged in criminal behavior, individuals might find themselves in environments that perpetuate the cycle. These environments often lack supportive social networks, access to resources, and opportunities for positive change (Lauritsen et al., 2014). The perpetuation of criminal behavior, then, further exposes individuals to traumatic experiences within the criminal justice system, perpetuating the cycle and making it difficult to break free from criminal involvement (Moffitt et al., 2002).

Breaking free from the cycle of developmental trauma and criminal behavior requires a comprehensive approach that addresses both individual and systemic factors. Therapeutic interventions, such as trauma-focused cognitive behavioral therapy (TF-CBT) or dialectical behavior therapy (DBT), can help individuals develop healthier coping strategies, address trauma-related symptoms, and learn prosocial skills. In addition, providing support services that address substance abuse treatment, education, job training, and housing can enhance the chances of successful reintegration into society.

3.4 Conclusion

The cycle of developmental trauma and criminal behavior is a complex and challenging pattern to break free from. Developmental trauma contributes to the development of criminal behavior, while the perpetuating factors of negative environments and risk factors further reinforce the connection. Understanding the intricate relationship between developmental trauma and criminal behavior is crucial for effective prevention and intervention strategies. By addressing the root causes, implementing trauma-informed care, providing early interventions, promoting healthy attachment relationships, and addressing comorbid psychopathology, we can mitigate the detrimental impact of developmental trauma and break the cycle of criminal behavior and achieve positive outcomes.

References

Ainsworth, M. D. S., Blehar, M. C., Waters, E., & Wall, S. N. (2015). *Patterns of attachment: A psychological study of the strange situation*. Psychology Press.

Bandura, A. (1973). Aggression: A social learning analysis. prentice-hall.

Bowlby, J. (1969). *Attachment and Loss* (Vol. 1). Attachment. Basic Books.

Bowlby, J. (1988). *A secure base: Parent-child attachment and healthy human development*. Basic Books.

Briere, J., Scott, C., & Weathers, F. (2005). Peritraumatic and persistent dissociation in the presumed etiology of PTSD. *American Journal of Psychiatry, 162*(12), 2295–2301.

Cohen, J. A., Mannarino, A. P., & Deblinger, E. (2016). *Treating trauma and traumatic grief in children and adolescents*. Guilford Press.

Covington, S. (2022). Creating a Trauma-informed justice system for women. In *The Wiley handbook on what works with girls and women in conflict with the law: A critical review of theory, practice, and policy* (pp. 172–184). Wiley.

Crittenden, P. M., & Spieker, S. J. (2018). Dynamic-maturational model of attachment and adaptation versus ABC+ D assessments of attachment in child protection and treatment: Reply to van IJzendoorn, Bakermans, steele, & Granqvist (2018). *Infant Mental Health Journal, 39*(6), 647–651.

Cullen, F. T. (1994). Social support as an organizing concept for criminology: Presidential address to the Academy of Criminal Justice Sciences. *Justice Quarterly, 11*(4), 527–559.

DeCandia, C., & Guarino, K. (2020). Trauma-informed care: An ecological response. *Journal of Child and Youth Care Work, 25*, 7–32. https://doi.org/10.5195/jcycw.2015.69

DeLisi, M., Piquero, A. R., & Cardwell, S. M. (2016). The unpredictability of murder: Juvenile homicide in the pathways to desistance study. *Youth Violence and Juvenile Justice, 14*(1), 26–42.

Fazel, S., Singh, J. P., Doll, H., & Grann, M. (2012). Use of risk assessment instruments to predict violence and antisocial behaviour in 73 samples involving 24 827 people: systematic review and meta-analysis. *BMJ, 345*.

Fonagy, P., Gergely, G., & Jurist, E. L. (2018). *Affect regulation, mentalization and the development of the self*. Routledge.

Ford, J. D., Grasso, D. J., Hawke, J., & Chapman, J. F. (2013). Poly-victimization among juvenile justice-involved youths. *Child Abuse & Neglect, 37*(10), 788–800.

Freud, S. (1961). *The Ego and the Id*. Norton.

Gold, A. L., Sheridan, M. A., Peverill, M., Busso, D. S., Lambert, H. K., Alves, S., Pine, D. S., & McLaughlin, K. A. (2016). Childhood abuse and reduced cortical thickness in brain regions involved in emotional processing. *Journal of Child Psychology and Psychiatry, 57*(10), 1154–1164.

Grossmann, K. E., & Grossmann, K. (2006). Attachment quality as an organizer of emotional and behavioral responses in a longitudinal perspective. In Attachment across the life cycle (pp. 101–122). Routledge.

Gvion, Y., & Apter, A. (2012). Suicide and suicidal behavior. *Public Health Reviews, 34*, 1–20.

Hofmann, W., Friese, M., & Wiers, R. W. (2008). Impulsive versus reflective influences on health behavior: A theoretical framework and empirical review. *Health Psychology Review, 2*(2), 111–137.

Kočovská, E., Puckering, C., & Follan, M. (2012). Attachment disorder behavior following early severe deprivation: Extension and longitudinal follow-up. *Journal of Abnormal Child Psychology, 40*(4), 689–700.

Laub, J. H., & Sampson, R. J. (2003). *Shared beginnings, divergent lives: Delinquent boys to age 70*. Harvard University Press.

Lauritsen, J. L., Rezey, M. L., & Heimer, K. (2014). Violence and economic conditions in the United States, 1973–2011: Gender, race, and ethnicity patterns in the National Crime Victimization Survey. *Journal of Contemporary Criminal Justice, 30*(1), 7–28.

Loeber, R., Farrington, D. P., Stouthamer-Loeber, M., & Van Kammen, W. B. (1998). *Antisocial behavior and mental health problems: Explanatory factors in childhood and adolescence*. Psychology Press.

Lyons-Ruth, K., & Jacobvitz, D. (2008). Attachment disorganization: Genetic factors, parenting contexts, and developmental transformation from infancy to adulthood. In J. Cassidy & P. R. Shaver (Eds.), *Handbook of attachment: Theory, research, and clinical applications* (2nd ed., pp. 666–697). The Guilford Press.

Lyons-Ruth, K., Alpern, L., & Repacholi, B. (1993). Disorganized infant attachment classification and maternal psychosocial problems as predictors of hostile-aggressive behavior in the preschool classroom. *Child Development, 64*(2), 572–585.

Lyons-Ruth, K., Bureau, J. F., Easterbrooks, M. A., Obsuth, I., Hennighausen, K., & Vulliez-Coady, L. (2016). Parsing the construct of maternal insensitivity: Distinct longitudinal pathways associated with early maternal withdrawal. *Maternal Sensitivity*, 120–140.

Main, M., & Hesse, E. (1990). Parents' unresolved traumatic experiences are related to infant disorganized attachment status: Is frightened and/or frightening parental behavior the linking mechanism? In M. T. Greenberg, D. Cicchetti, & E. M. Cummings (Eds.), *Attachment in the preschool years: Theory, research, and intervention* (pp. 161–182). University of Chicago Press.

Main, M., & Solomon, J. (1990). Procedures for identifying infants as disorganized/disoriented during the Ainsworth Strange Situation. In M. T. Greenberg, D. Cicchetti, & E. M. Cummings (Eds.), *Attachment in the preschool years: Theory, research, and intervention* (pp. 121–160). University of Chicago Press.

Main, M., Kaplan, N., & Cassidy, J. (1985). Security in infancy, childhood, and adulthood: A move to the level of representation. *Monographs of the Society for Research in Child Development*, 66–104.

Moffitt, T. E., & Caspi, A. (2001). Childhood predictors differentiate life-course persistent and adolescence-limited antisocial pathways among males and females. *Development and Psychopathology, 13*(2), 355–375.

Moffitt, T. E., Caspi, A., Harrington, H., & Milne, B. J. (2002). Males on the life-course-persistent and adolescence-limited antisocial pathways: Follow-up at age 26 years. *Development and Psychopathology, 14*(1), 179–207.

Moran, G., Vuchinich, S., & Hall, N. (2004). Associations between types of maltreatment and substance use during adolescence. *Child Abuse & Neglect, 28*(5), 565–574.

Otasowie, J. (2021). Co-occurring mental disorder and substance use disorder in young people: aetiology, assessment and treatment. *BJPsych Advances, 27*(4), 272–281. https://doi.org/10.1192/bja.2020.64

Perry, B. D. (2002). Childhood experience and the expression of genetic potential: What childhood neglect tells us about nature and nurture. *Brain and Mind, 3*(02), 79–100.

Reijntjes, A., Kamphuis, J. H., Prinzie, P., & Telch, M. J. (2010). Peer victimization and internalizing problems in children: A meta-analysis of longitudinal studies. *Child Abuse & Neglect, 34*(4), 244–252.

Schore, A. N. (2001). The effects of early relational trauma on right brain development, affect regulation, and infant mental health. *Infant Mental Health Journal, 22*(1–2), 201–269.

Smith, C. A., & Thornberry, T. P. (1995). The relationship between childhood maltreatment and adolescent involvement in delinquency. *Criminology, 33*(4), 451–481.

Spinazzola, J., Hodgdon, H., Liang, L.-J., Ford, J. D., Layne, C. M., Pynoos, R., Briggs, E. C., Stolbach, B., & Kisiel, C. (2014). Unseen wounds: The contribution of psychological maltreatment to child and adolescent mental health and risk outcomes. *Psychological Trauma: Theory, Research, Practice, and Policy, 6*(Suppl 1), S18–S28. https://doi.org/10.1037/a0037766

Teicher, M. H., Samson, J. A., Anderson, C. M., & Ohashi, K. (2016). The effects of childhood maltreatment on brain structure, function and connectivity. *Nature Reviews Neuroscience, 17*(10), 652–666.

Thornberry, T. P., Ireland, T. O., & Smith, C. A. (2001). The importance of timing: The varying impact of childhood and adolescent maltreatment on multiple problem outcomes. *Development and Psychopathology, 13*(4), 957–979.

van Ijzendoorn, M. H., Schuengel, C., & Bakermans-Kranenburg, M. J. (1999). Disorganized attachment in early childhood: Meta-analysis of precursors, concomitants, and sequelae. *Development and Psychopathology, 11*(2), 225–250.

Widom, C. S. (1989). The cycle of violence. *Science, 244*(4901), 160–166.

Wright, B. R., Caspi, A., Moffitt, T. E., & Paternoster, R. (2004). Does the perceived risk of punishment deter criminally prone individuals? Rational choice, self-control, and crime. *Journal of Research in Crime and Delinquency, 41*(2), 180–213.

Chapter 4
Trauma-Informed Approaches in the Criminal Justice System

The criminal justice system has traditionally focused on punishment as a means of deterring crime and promoting public safety. However, there is a growing recognition that many individuals who enter the system have experienced significant trauma in their lives, which has often played a contributing role in their involvement in criminal activities. The concept of trauma-informed care is gaining prominence as a transformative approach within the criminal justice system, one that acknowledges the impact of trauma and works to create an environment that is supportive, rehabilitative, and seeks to address the root causes of criminal behavior. This chapter aims to provide a comprehensive analysis of trauma-informed approaches within the criminal justice system, focusing specifically on offender rehabilitation programs. It explores how trauma-informed care can be effectively incorporated into rehabilitation programs, the importance of understanding and addressing trauma histories in the assessment and treatment of offenders, and evidence-based practices that promote trauma-informed principles within correctional settings. By integrating trauma-informed approaches into the criminal justice system, it is hoped that individuals can heal from their past traumas, find pathways to rehabilitation, and foster a safer and more inclusive society.

4.1 Understanding Trauma and the Criminal Justice System

Traumatic experiences can have a profound impact on individuals, affecting their mental health, behavior, and overall well-being. The criminal justice system, designed to maintain law and order, often intersects with individuals who have experienced trauma. Recognizing the prevalence and impact of trauma is essential for developing effective approaches with the criminal justice system that promotes healing, rehabilitation, and the prevention of reoffending.

K. Sapp, *Exploring Developmental Trauma Disorder Among Offending Populations*, SpringerBriefs in Offending Populations & Correctional Psychotherapy,
https://doi.org/10.1007/978-3-031-61157-5_4

4.1.1 Definition and Types of Trauma

Trauma can be defined as an event or experience that overwhelms an individual's ability to cope and negatively impacts their psychological, emotional, or physical well-being (Fallot & Harris, 2008). Trauma can take various forms, including but not limited to:

1. Acute Trauma: This refers to a single traumatic event, such as a physical assault, natural disaster, or witnessing a violent incident (Kessler et al., 2013).
2. Chronic Trauma: This type of trauma often occurs repeatedly over an extended period and includes experiences such as ongoing abuse, neglect, or living in a war-torn area.
3. Complex Trauma: Complex trauma results from exposure to multiple traumatic experiences, usually beginning in childhood, involving interpersonal violence, and often within the context of a trusted relationship (Courtois & Ford, 2009).

4.1.2 Types of Traumas Experienced

Trauma experienced by justice-involved individuals can take various forms. Common types of traumas include:

1. Physical and Sexual Abuse: Many individuals involved in the criminal justice system have experienced physical or sexual abuse during childhood or adulthood (Briere & Scott, 2012). Research has consistently shown a strong association between childhood abuse and subsequent criminal behavior (Widom, 1989).
2. Community Violence: Justice-involved individuals are often exposed to community violence, including witnessing or being victims of assaults, shootings, or gang-related activities (Ford et al., 2007). This exposure can lead to significant psychological distress and trauma-related symptoms.
3. Neglect and Emotional Abuse: Neglect and emotional abuse during childhood contribute to the development of trauma among justice-involved individuals (Ford et al., 2007). The lack of nurturing and support can have long-lasting effects on their psychological well-being and behavior.

4.1.3 Effects of Trauma on Individuals

Trauma can have a wide range of effects on individuals, impacting various aspects of their lives. The effects can manifest in physical, psychological, emotional, and behavioral symptoms. Some common effects of trauma include:

1. Post-Traumatic Stress Disorder (PTSD): PTSD is a psychological disorder that can develop after experiencing a traumatic event or series of events. Symptoms

may include flashbacks, nightmares, hyperarousal, and avoidance of triggers (American Psychiatric Association, 2013).
2. Substance Abuse: Many individuals turn to substance abuse as a coping mechanism to numb their emotional pain resulting from trauma (Kilpatrick et al., 2013).
3. Revictimization and Criminality: Trauma can increase the risk of engaging in criminal behavior as individuals may resort to coping strategies such as aggression or involvement in illegal activities (Widom, 1989).

4.2 Prevalence of Trauma Among Justice Involved Individuals

Justice-involved individuals, such as offenders and ex-offenders, often bear the weight of traumatic experiences in their lives. Research consistently shows that a significant proportion of individuals within the criminal justice system have experienced trauma. For example, a study conducted by Ford et al. (2010) found that approximately 93% of youth involved in the criminal justice system have experienced at least one traumatic event in their lifetime. The study titled, "Trauma among youth in the juvenile justice system: Critical issues and new directions" aimed to investigate the prevalence of trauma among youth involved in the juvenile justice system. The researchers recognized the importance of understanding the trauma experiences of these young individuals and how it might impact their behavior and rehabilitation outcomes. To gather data, the researchers administered trauma assessments to a sample of youth within the juvenile justice system. The study participants were naked about their exposure to various traumatic events, such as physical and sexual abuse, community violence, neglect, and emotional abuse. The findings of the study revealed substantial rates of trauma among the youth involved in the juvenile justice system. The high prevalence indicated a significant burden of trauma among the juvenile justice population. Furthermore, the study highlighted the interplay between trauma and juvenile delinquency. The researchers were able to identify a strong association between trauma exposure and subsequent involvement in delinquent behaviors.

Childhood trauma plays a crucial role in the development of criminal behaviors. Considering that the link between childhood trauma and later engagement in criminal activity has long been a topic of research and debate, Mersky et al. (2013) conducted a significant cohort study to investigate the influence of childhood trauma on criminal involvement in adulthood. The researchers utilized an urban, minority sample in the United States and examined the impact of adverse childhood experiences (ACEs) on health, mental health, and substance use in early adulthood.

The study revealed a compelling association between childhood trauma and the heightened risk of engaging in criminal activities later in life. The researchers identified several key findings within their investigation:

1. Adverse Childhood Experiences (ACEs) and Criminal Engagement:

The study found that individuals with a history of childhood trauma, represented by adverse childhood experiences (ACEs), exhibit an increased likelihood of involvement in criminal behavior during adulthood. The higher the number of ACEs reported, the stronger the association with criminality.

2. Types of Traumas and Criminal Behavior:

Different types of childhood trauma, such as physical abuse, sexual abuse, neglect, or household dysfunction, were assessed for their influence on criminal engagement. The researchers identified specific ACE subcategories that were significantly correlated with criminal involvement, providing insight into the potential mechanisms behind the association.

3. Mediating Factors:

The study highlighted the role of various mediating factors in the relationship between childhood trauma and criminal behavior. Factors such as mental health issues, substance abuse, and difficulties in forming healthy relationships were identified as potential links that contribute to the pathway from childhood trauma to criminal engagement.

The findings of the study conducted by Mersky et al. (2013) have significant implications for understanding and addressing the issue of criminal behavior in individuals with a history of childhood trauma. Several key implications emerge from their research:

1. Early Identification and Intervention:

Identifying children who have experienced trauma and providing appropriate interventions can be crucial in preventing future criminal involvement. Early identification allows for targeted support, including counseling, therapy, and other intervention strategies, to mitigate the negative effects of trauma and break the cycle of criminal behavior.

2. Trauma-Informed Criminal Justice System:

The study emphasizes the need for a trauma-informed approach within the criminal justice system. Recognizing the impact of childhood trauma on individuals involved in the justice system can facilitate more effective rehabilitation programs, tailored to address trauma-related issues and reduce reoffending rates.

3. Targeted Support Services:

The research underscores the importance of providing comprehensive support services to individuals with a history of childhood trauma. Engaging in trauma-focused therapies, ensuring access to mental health treatment, and offering social support can aid in healing, reducing the likelihood of future criminal behavior.

Ultimately, the study conducted by Mersky et al. (2013) provides compelling evidence supporting the association between childhood trauma and the increased likelihood of engaging in criminal behavior later in life. Understanding this relationship has vital implications for interventions, policies, and programs aimed at reducing the risk of criminal involvement and promoting healing and rehabilitation among individuals with a history of childhood trauma.

Furthermore, justice-involved individuals, during their time in correctional facilities are often exposed to environments that may retraumatize them. This includes witnessing violence, experiencing physical or sexual assault, and enduring harsh living conditions. Fazel et al. (2016) conducted a comprehensive research review to examine the prevalence of traumatic experiences among prisoners. Their research focused on exploring the histories of trauma exposure in a sample of incarcerated individuals, shedding light on the extent of traumatic incidents within this population.

The research by Fazel et al. (2016) revealed disturbingly high rates of traumatic experiences among prisoners. The key findings of their investigation are outlined below:

1. Prevalence of Traumatic Experiences:

More than half of the prisoners surveyed reported a history of traumatic experiences. This indicates that a substantial proportion of the incarcerated population has gone through significant traumas in their lives.

2. Types of Traumas:

The study considered various forms of trauma, including physical abuse, sexual abuse, emotional abuse, neglect, and witnessing violence. The participants reported experiencing one or multiple forms of trauma, highlighting the diverse traumatic backgrounds prevalent among prisoners.

3. Prevalence of Post-Traumatic Stress Disorder (PTSD):

The study also assessed the prevalence of post-traumatic stress disorder (PTSD) among prisoners with a history of traumatic experiences. The findings indicated that a significant number of prisoners met the criteria for a PTSD diagnosis, further underscoring the mental health consequences of trauma within this population.

The research conducted by Fazel et al. (2016) also holds important implications for understanding and addressing the needs of prisoners with a history of traumatic experiences. Several key implications emerge from their research:

1. Trauma-Informed Correctional Practices:

The findings highlight the necessity of trauma-informed practices within correctional settings. Incorporating trauma-informed approaches can enhance the well-being of prisoners by creating a supportive and safe environment that acknowledges and addresses the effects of trauma.

2. Mental Health Support:

The high prevalence of traumatic experiences among prisoners emphasizes the need for comprehensive mental health support within correctional facilities. Access to trauma-informed therapies, counseling services, and appropriate treatment for PTSD can aid in facilitating the healing and recovery process.

3. Tailored Reentry Programs:

Recognizing the impact of trauma on incarcerated individuals is crucial when designing reentry programs. Tailored support services that address trauma-related needs can strengthen successful reintegration into society, reduce recidivism rates, and promote overall well-being.

Overall, the research conducted by Fazel et al. (2016) sheds light on the alarming prevalence of traumatic experiences among prisoners. Understanding the high rates of trauma within this population is essential for developing trauma-informed approaches, providing mental health support, and designing effective reentry programs that can contribute to the rehabilitation and well-being of incarcerated individuals.

4.3 The Concept of Trauma-Informed Care

Trauma-informed care, a concept gaining recognition in healthcare and social service settings, reflects a paradigm shift in addressing the needs of individuals who have experienced trauma. According to the Substance Abuse and Mental Health Services Administration (SAMHSA), trauma-informed care is an approach that recognizes and responds to the widespread impact of trauma, while seeking to prevent all aspects of re-traumatization (2014). It acknowledges the prevalence of trauma and integrates knowledge about trauma into policies, practices, and procedures.

4.3.1 Benefits of a Trauma Informed Approach

1. Avoidance of Re-traumatization:

   Trauma-informed care emphasizes the creation of safe and respectful environments where individuals feel supported, heard, and validated. By avoiding practices that may inadvertently trigger trauma responses, the risk of re-traumatization is reduced, promoting healing and recovery (SAMHSA, 2014).
2. Improved Treatment Outcomes:

   By recognizing the impact of trauma on individuals' physical and mental health, trauma-informed care aims to tailor interventions and treatments to address trauma-related needs. This individualized approach can enhance treatment engagement, adherence, and overall outcomes (SAMHSA, 2014).
3. Enhanced Collaborative Relationships:

   Trauma-informed care seeks to establish collaborative relationships between service providers and individuals. This approach encourages active involvement, shared decision-making, and the cultivation of trusting partnerships, fostering a sense of empowerment and respect (SAMHSA, 2014).

4.3.2 Applications of Trauma-Informed Care

1. Health and Mental Health Settings:
   Trauma-informed care has been implemented in various healthcare settings, including hospitals, community health centers, and mental health clinics. It informs the delivery of medical and mental health services by addressing the unique needs of trauma survivors and creating a supportive and healing environment (SAMHSA, 2014).
2. Social Services and Advocacy:
   Social service organizations, such as shelters, child welfare agencies, and victim advocacy programs, have embraced trauma-informed care as a way to better meet the needs of their clients. This approach recognizes the systemic impact of trauma and guides organizations to provide trauma-sensitive services and support (SAMHSA, 2014).
3. Education and Workplaces:
   Trauma-informed principles are increasingly being applied in educational settings, including schools and universities. By understanding the effects of trauma on students, educators can create safe and supportive learning environments that foster resilience and academic success. Additionally, trauma-informed practices are being adopted in workplaces to promote employee well-being and productivity (SAMHSA, 2014).

4.4 Importance of Trauma-Informed Approaches in Correctional Setting

Implementing trauma-informed approaches in correctional settings is crucial for addressing the needs of incarcerated individuals who have experienced trauma. Correctional institutions have the potential to inadvertently retraumatize the offending population if they do not employ trauma-informed approaches. Trauma-informed approaches recognize that trauma shapes an individual's behaviors and responses. By understanding the underlying trauma, correctional staff can address the key core principles, to include safety, trust, empowerment, and collaboration/choice (SAMHSA, 2014). As such, trauma-informed approaches focus on creating an environment that is sensitive, supportive, and responsive to the needs of individuals who have experienced trauma (Fallot & Harris, 2008). This approach can facilitate behavior change, reduce violence, and promote positive outcomes both during incarceration and upon reentry into society.

Key Core Principles of Trauma-Informed Care

1. **Safety:** Creating a sense of physical and emotional safety within correctional settings is essential for individuals with trauma histories (Grella et al., 2005).
2. **Trust:** Establishing trust between criminal justice professionals and individuals is vital to create a supportive environment where trauma-related issues can be addressed (Briere & Scott, 2012).
3. **Empowerment:** Trauma-informed approaches aim to empower individuals by involving them in decision-making processes and promoting their autonomy (Mills et al., 2006).
4. **Collaboration and Choice:** Involving individuals in their own treatment planning and providing choices promotes a sense of control and ownership in their rehabilitation process (Bloom, 2013).

Research supports the efficacy of trauma-informed approaches in reducing mental health issues, disciplinary problems, and violence among incarcerated individuals, highlighting the significance of integrating trauma-informed care into correctional systems. As mentioned earlier, the study by Fazel et al. (2016) supports the importance of trauma-informed approaches within correctional settings. Their research highlighted the high prevalence of trauma and PTSD among prisoners, emphasizing the need for specialized care.

Chaudhri et al. (2019) literature review provides valuable insights into the benefits of trauma-informed care in correctional settings. The review synthesized existing research and highlighted the positive outcomes associated with trauma-informed practices within correctional institutions. Chaudhri emphasized the importance of recognizing the prevalence and impact of trauma, as well as the need to implement trauma-informed approaches to improve outcomes for incarcerated individuals.

Key Findings and Implications of Chaudhri et al. (2019) Literature Review

1. Improved Mental Health Outcomes:

Chaudhri et al. (2019) review highlighted that trauma-informed care in correctional settings can lead to improved mental health outcomes among incarcerated individuals. Trauma-specific therapies and counseling services that address the underlying trauma can help reduce symptoms of post-traumatic stress disorder (PTSD) and other mental health issues.

The implementation of trauma-informed approaches recognizes the impact of trauma on incarcerated individuals' mental health and provides appropriate support. This can lead to a reduction in psychiatric symptoms, better emotional regulation, and an improved sense of well-being among incarcerated individuals (Chaudhri et al., 2019).

2. Reduced Disciplinary Problems:

An essential benefit of trauma-informed care in correctional settings, as revealed by Chaudhri et al. (2019), is the potential to reduce disciplinary problems among incarcerated individuals. Trauma-informed approaches prioritize understanding the underlying trauma and the impact it may have on behavior and coping strategies. By addressing these factors, correctional institutions can employ interventions that reduce aggression, self-harm, and other behavioral issues.

3. Decreased Violence:

Chaudhri et al. (2019) literature review highlighted that trauma-informed care can contribute to a decrease in violence within correctional settings. By recognizing the role of trauma in shaping behavior and providing appropriate support and interventions, trauma-informed care aims to create a safer and more supportive environment. This approach fosters trust, helps individuals develop healthier coping skills, and reduces the likelihood of aggressive or violent interactions.

4. Increased Client Satisfaction:

Implementing trauma-informed care in correctional settings appears to contribute to increased client satisfaction among incarcerated individuals (Chaudhri et al., 2019). The adoption of trauma-informed practices establishes a culture of respect, empathy, and understanding, creating an environment where individuals feel valued and supported. This improved sense of well-being and positive interactions with staff members can enhance overall satisfaction with their experience in the correctional system.

Ultimately, Chaudhri et al. (2019) literature review provides compelling evidence for the benefits of trauma-informed care in correctional settings. By addressing the impact of trauma and integrating trauma-informed approaches, correctional institutions can improve mental health outcomes, reduce disciplinary problems, decrease violence, and increase client satisfaction among incarcerated individuals. Therefore, in conclusion, understanding trauma and its impact is crucial within the criminal justice system to address the underlying factors contributing to criminal behavior and to promote rehabilitation. By recognizing the prevalence and impact of trauma, correctional institutions can create environments that support healing, reduce re-traumatization, and promote successful rehabilitation.

4.5 Key Components of Establishing Trauma-Informed Correctional Settings

The creation of a trauma-informed correctional setting involves a comprehensive transformation of policies, practices, and culture to address the needs of offending populations who have experienced trauma. Research has consistently revealed high rates of trauma among offending populations and unaddressed trauma can impede the success of rehabilitative efforts. To enhance rehabilitative efforts and influence the reduction in recidivism rates, trauma-informed must be integrated into correctional settings. This section will discuss strategies for policy development, implementation of trauma-informed practices, and the importance of fostering a supportive and empathetic culture among correctional settings.

4.5.1 Policy Development for Trauma-Informed Care

The development of trauma-informed policies plays a crucial role in creating correctional settings that promote trauma-informed care. These policies provide the framework for identifying, understanding, and responding to the impact of trauma on offending populations (Briere et al., 2015). By adopting trauma-informed policy frameworks and incorporating trauma-specific screening assessment tools, correctional settings can ensure that trauma-related needs are being addressed effectively.

4.5.1.1 Trauma-Informed Policy Framework

Correctional settings are faced with the challenge of addressing the complex needs of offending populations who have experienced trauma across their lifespans. Trauma-inflicted individuals are particularly vulnerable and require specialized care to promote healing, rehabilitation, and overall well-being. The adoption of trauma-informed policy frameworks acknowledges the prevalence and significant impact of trauma within the correctional population. Trauma-informed policies ensure that correctional systems recognize the traumatic experiences that many incarcerated individuals have endured and the subsequent effects on their emotional well-being, behavior, and overall functioning (Briere et al., 2015). By acknowledging and understanding trauma, policies can guide correctional environments to provide specialized support and interventions tailored to address the deeply rooted trauma-related needs of individuals.

Trauma-informed policy frameworks prioritize healing and rehabilitation as central objectives within correctional settings. By integrating trauma-informed principles into policies, these frameworks promote interventions and practices that align with evidence-based strategies for trauma recovery (Miller & Najavits, 2012). In doing so, they encourage the implementation of trauma-specific interventions, such as Cognitive Behavioral Therapy for Trauma (CBT-T), which have been proven effective in reducing trauma symptoms and facilitating healing among incarcerated populations (Briere et al., 2015). By prioritizing healing, trauma-informed policies contribute to the overall rehabilitation and successful reintegration of offending populations.

Addressing trauma-related needs within correctional settings is vital to prevent re-traumatization. Adopting trauma-informed policy frameworks ensures that correctional environments are designed to minimize potential triggers and avoid practices that may exacerbate trauma symptoms. Trauma-informed policies prioritize the creation of safe and secure environments that foster trust, communication, and effective therapeutic relationships (Miller & Najavits, 2012). By creating a trauma-informed culture, correctional staff can interact with incarcerated individuals in a supportive and empathic manner, reducing the likelihood of re-traumatization and enabling healing to occur (Briere et al., 2015).

Trauma-informed policy frameworks highlight the importance of staff competence and training in addressing the trauma-related needs of incarcerated populations. Policies mandate comprehensive training for correctional staff, including education on trauma awareness, trauma-informed principles, and the impact of trauma on behavior (Miller & Najavits, 2012). Training helps staff develop the skills and knowledge necessary to respond empathetically and effectively to incarcerated individuals who have experienced trauma. Staff who are equipped with trauma-informed training can play a crucial role in supporting healing, promoting a sense of safety, and facilitating the overall well-being of offenders with trauma histories.

In conclusion, the adoption of trauma-informed policies within correctional settings is a critical step towards creating healing-centered environments that prioritize the well-being, rehabilitation, and successful reintegration of offending populations with trauma histories. These policies recognize the impact of trauma, promote healing and rehabilitation, prevent re-traumatization, and enhance staff competence in addressing trauma-related needs. By integrating trauma-informed policy frameworks, correctional systems can create environments that foster healing, empower individuals, and contribute to overall positive outcomes for both incarcerated individuals and society.

4.5.1.2 Adoption of Trauma-Informed Screening and Assessment

Adopting trauma-informed policy frameworks that emphasize screening and assessment is of the utmost importance in correctional settings for offending populations who have experienced trauma. Screening and assessment processes play a pivotal role in identifying and addressing the unique trauma-related histories and needs of offending populations. It is noted that these assessments help inform treatment planning and interventions based on individual needs. Ultimately, proper trauma screening and assessment supports the creation of personalized care plans within a trauma-informed framework (Briere et al., 2015).

4.5.1.2.1 Addressing Trauma Histories in Offender Assessment and Treatment

Addressing trauma histories in offender assessment and treatment is crucial for promoting effective rehabilitation and reducing recidivism rates among offending populations. Many offenders have experienced traumatic events that contribute to their involvement in criminal behavior. Failing to address these underlying traumas can hinder the success of rehabilitation efforts. Incorporating trauma-informed approaches in offender assessment and treatment requires the recognition of trauma histories. Many studies indicate a high prevalence of trauma among offending populations, often linked to adverse childhood experiences or exposure to violence (Ford et al., 2015).

Components and General Outline of Trauma History Assessments
Gathering Trauma History

The assessment should collect a comprehensive inventory of traumatic events offending populations have experienced throughout their lives, include but not limited to the nature and timing of the traumatic events (Van der Kolk, 2014):

Explore different types of traumatic events, including physical or sexual abuse, accidents, natural disasters, combat exposure, etc.

Collect information on the age or developmental stage at the time of each event.

Inquire about key details such as duration, severity, and perceived threat.

Assessing Trauma Symptoms Impact

It is essential to evaluate the impact of trauma on offending populations psychological well-being and overall functioning. This involves assessing symptoms of trauma and impairments in daily functioning (American Psychiatric Association, 2013).

Trauma Symptoms:

Assess trauma-related symptoms such as intrusive thoughts, nightmares, flashbacks, distressing memories, or physiological reactions associated with traumatic events.

Evaluate symptoms of avoidance, including efforts to avoid reminders of trauma, numbing, or emotional detachment.

Inquire about alterations in mood and cognition, such as negative beliefs about oneself, distorted blame or guilt, or diminished interest in activities.

Evaluate hyperarousal symptoms, including irritability, hypervigilance, difficulty concentrating, or exaggerated startle response.

(continued)

Impact of Trauma:

Assess the impact of trauma on different domains of functioning, such as work or school, relationships, and overall quality of life.

Evaluate potential difficulties in emotional regulation, interpersonal relationships, self-esteem, or trust.

Inquire about any changes in behavior patterns, such as substance use, self-harm, or risky behaviors.

Risk and Protective Factors

Assessing potential risk factors and protective factors provides insight into the offending population's resources with dealing with traumatic experiences (Hobfoll et al., 2007) as well as understanding of their vulnerability to trauma-related symptoms (Scott et al., 2012).

Explore protective factors such as social support, coping skills, and resilience that have helped the individual manage trauma-related distress.

Assess potential risk factors including ongoing exposure to trauma, lack of social support, or comorbid mental health conditions.

Screening for Additional Mental Health Concerns:

Assess other common mental health concerns that may co-occur with trauma, such as depression, anxiety, substance use, or dissociative symptoms.

Note: Remember, it is important to use trauma-informed and culturally sensitive approaches when conducting a trauma history assessment. Depending on your specific context or purpose, it may be helpful to seek guidance from mental health professionals or consult established trauma assessment tools and guidelines.

By acknowledging the impact of trauma, assessment methods can seek to identify trauma-related symptoms, such as post-traumatic stress disorder (PTSD), dissociation, or substance abuse, that may hinder progress during rehabilitation (Miller & Najavits, 2012). Trauma-informed assessment tools, like the Clinician-Administered PTSD Scale for DSM-5 (CAPS-5), Trauma Symptom Inventory (TSI), and the Trauma History Questionnaire (THQ), have been developed to identify trauma histories and inform appropriate treatment strategies (Weathers et al., 2018; Briere, 1997, Green, 1996). Recognizing trauma as a contributing factor allows for a targeted approach to offender intervention and treatment.

Clinician-Administered PTSD Scale for DSM-5 (CAPS-5)

The Clinician-Administered PTSD Scale for DSM-5 (CAPS-5) is widely recognized as the gold standard for assessing post-traumatic stress disorder (PTSD) symptoms in adults (Weathers et al., 2013). It is a structured interview administered by trained clinicians to determine the presence and severity of PTSD symptoms based on the DSM-5 diagnostic criteria.

CAPS-5 focuses on the four symptom clusters associated with PTSD: intrusion, avoidance, negative alterations in cognition and mood, and alterations in arousal and reactivity. The assessment consists of questions regarding the nature and frequency of traumatic events, subjective distress related to trauma, and the impact of symptoms on various aspects of functioning (Weathers et al., 2013).

During the interview, the clinician rates each symptom item on a severity scale to ascertain the frequency and intensity of the individual's symptoms (Weathers et al., 2013). CAPS-5 also includes sections to assess dissociative symptoms and other PTSD-related specifications, such as delayed expression (Weathers et al., 2013).

The standardized and comprehensive nature of CAPS-5 makes it invaluable for diagnosing PTSD and developing individualized treatment plans (Weathers et al., 2013). The utilization of CAPS-5 results in consistent assessments and facilitates monitoring symptom changes over time, evaluating treatment effectiveness, and ensuring appropriate care for individuals affected by trauma.

Reference

Weathers, F. W., Litz, B. T., Keane, T. M., Palmieri, P. A., Marx, B. P., & Schnurr, P. P. (2013). *The PTSD Checklist for DSM-5 (PCL-5) – Standard*. National Center for PTSD.

Trauma Symptom Inventory (TSI)

The Trauma Symptom Inventory (TSI) is a widely used assessment tool designed to evaluate trauma-related symptoms and their impact on an individual's functioning. Developed by Briere (1997), the TSI assesses a range of symptoms commonly associated with trauma, including anxiety, depression, dissociation, sexual concerns, sleep disturbances, and somatic complaints.

The TSI consists of 100 self-report items that measure various psychological and behavioral symptoms related to trauma. Individuals rate the frequency and severity of each symptom they have experienced over a defined timeframe. The assessment yields scores in different symptom domains, allowing clinicians to identify specific areas of distress and tailor treatment accordingly.

(continued)

The TSI covers a comprehensive range of trauma-related symptoms, making it useful for assessing the impact of trauma on an individual's mental health and overall well-being. It provides valuable information for treatment planning, as it helps clinicians identify specific symptoms that require attention and guide interventions.

Furthermore, the TSI allows for the evaluation of symptom severity and monitoring of changes over time. By administering the TSI at multiple points in treatment, clinicians can track progress and adjust interventions, accordingly, ensuring that the treatment is effective and addressing the individual's needs.

The TSI has been widely used in research and clinical settings, providing valuable insights into trauma-related symptoms and their impact on individuals' lives (Briere, 1997). Its holistic approach in assessing various trauma-related domains contributes to a comprehensive understanding of an individual's trauma-related difficulties, leading to more targeted and effective interventions.

Reference

Briere, J. (1997). *Trauma Symptom Inventory (TSI) Professional Manual.* Psychological Assessment Resources.

Trauma History Questionnaire (THQ)

The Trauma History Questionnaire (THQ), developed by Green (1996), is a widely used assessment tool designed to gather comprehensive information about an individual's exposure to traumatic events throughout their lifetime.

The THQ is a self-report measure that consists of a series of questions that assess various types of traumatic events. It covers a broad range of potentially traumatic experiences, including physical and sexual abuse, accidents, natural disasters, witnessing violence, and other distressing events. The questionnaire assesses the frequency of exposure to these events, as well as the age at which they occurred.

By gathering detailed information about an individual's trauma history, the THQ helps clinicians and researchers gain a deeper understanding of the scope and nature of an individual's trauma exposure. This information is essential for accurately assessing the impact of trauma on an individual's mental health and overall well-being.

The THQ is valuable in clinical and research settings as it provides a systematic approach to identifying and quantifying traumatic experiences. Clinicians can use the THQ to guide treatment planning, ensuring that interventions are tailored to address the specific traumatic experiences that have contributed to an individual's distress. Researchers can utilize the THQ to

(continued)

study the relationship between trauma exposure and various psychological outcomes, aiding in the development of evidence-based interventions.

The THQ has demonstrated good reliability and validity in assessing trauma history and is widely used in the field of trauma research and clinical practice (Green, 1996). Its comprehensive nature and standardized format make it an important tool for gathering information about an individual's lifetime exposure to traumatic events.

Addressing trauma histories within offender assessment and treatment involves tailoring interventions to target trauma-related symptoms. Traditional rehabilitation approaches may not effectively address the underlying trauma that drives criminal behavior. Trauma-informed treatment frameworks prioritize evidence-based practices such as Trauma-Focused Cognitive-Behavioral Therapy (TF-CBT) or Eye Movement Desensitization and Reprocessing (EMDR) to address trauma-related symptoms and facilitate healing (Gould et al., 1997). These trauma-specific interventions aim to reduce trauma symptoms, enhance coping skills, and promote healthy behavioral changes necessary for successful rehabilitation.

A trauma-informed approach to offender assessment and treatment also involves creating a safe and supportive environment that fosters healing. Correctional settings must prioritize the emotional and physical safety of individuals who have experienced trauma. Staff should receive training on trauma-informed care, promoting empathy, trust-building, and respect in their interactions with incarcerated individuals (Drescher, 2018). Establishing a trauma-informed culture helps offenders feel validated, reducing the re-traumatization that can occur within traditional punitive systems (Miller & Najavits, 2012). Collaborative efforts among correctional staff, mental health professionals, and support services are essential in creating an environment conducive to healing and promoting overall well-being.

An essential aspect of addressing trauma histories in offender assessment and treatment is ongoing evaluation and monitoring of treatment progress. Trauma-informed policies emphasize the importance of regularly assessing the effectiveness of interventions and modifying treatment plans as necessary (Ford et al., 2015). Monitoring trauma-specific symptoms, changes in coping mechanisms, and overall functioning allows for adjustments in treatment approaches to ensure optimal outcomes. Evaluation conducted by trained professionals using validated measures, such as the Posttraumatic Stress Disorder Checklist (PCL-5) or the Trauma Symptom Inventory (TSI), provides valuable insights into an individual's progress and guides subsequent interventions (Briere, 1995).

In conclusion, addressing trauma histories in offender assessment and treatment is vital for promoting effective rehabilitation within correctional settings. By incorporating trauma-informed approaches, recognizing trauma histories, tailoring interventions, creating a safe and supportive environment, and continuously evaluating treatment progress, correctional systems can enhance the well-being and rehabilitation outcomes of incarcerated individuals with traumatic experiences. A commitment to trauma-informed practices provides an opportunity for healing, minimizing the risk of re-traumatization, and facilitating successful reintegration into society.

4.5.1.2.2 Case Analysis: Significance of Trauma-Informed Assessment Tools and Techniques

Trauma-informed assessment tools and techniques play a crucial role in identifying trauma-related symptoms, improving treatment planning, and mitigating the risk of re-traumatization among individuals who have experienced trauma. This case analysis aims to explore the significance of trauma-informed assessment in a hypothetical case study, illustrating the positive outcomes and benefits of utilizing these tools and techniques.

The Case of Sarah

Sarah, a 27-year-old woman with a history of domestic violence and childhood abuse, seeks therapy due to recurring nightmares, hypervigilance, and difficulty trusting others. Understanding the importance of trauma-informed care, Sarah's therapist employs trauma-informed assessment tools and techniques to facilitate a comprehensive evaluation.

Identification of Trauma-Related Symptoms:

Trauma-informed assessment tools, such as the Clinician-Administered PTSD Scale for DSM-5 (CAPS-5) or the Trauma Symptom Inventory (TSI), allow Sarah's therapist to accurately identify trauma-related symptoms (Weathers et al., 2018; Briere, 1997). Through a thorough evaluation, Sarah's symptoms, including flashbacks, avoidance behaviors, and emotional dysregulation, are assessed, providing insight into the impact of trauma on her mental health and overall well-being.

Improved Treatment Planning:

Trauma-informed assessment results serve as a foundation for developing an effective treatment plan tailored to Sarah's specific needs. By identifying trauma-related symptoms, Sarah's therapist can select evidence-based interventions that target the root causes of her distress. Trauma-focused therapies such as Cognitive Processing Therapy (CPT) or Prolonged Exposure (PE) may be recommended to address Sarah's traumatic experiences and reduce associated symptoms (Resick et al., 2006; Foa et al., 2007).

(continued)

Mitigation of Re-traumatization Risk:

Trauma-informed assessment tools and techniques also play a significant role in minimizing the risk of re-traumatization during the treatment process. Understanding Sarah's trauma history and adverse experiences enables her therapist to create a safe and supportive therapeutic environment. Implementing trauma-informed practices, such as establishing a trusting therapeutic relationship, providing psychoeducation about trauma, and utilizing grounding techniques, helps to ensure that Sarah feels respected, validated, and empowered throughout her treatment journey (Harris & Fallot, 2001; Najavits, 2002).

Monitoring Progress and Adjusting Treatment:

Trauma-informed assessment tools and techniques are not limited to the initial evaluation but also provide a means to monitor treatment progress and adjust interventions accordingly. Regular assessments using appropriate measures like the PTSD Checklist for DSM-5 (PCL-5) or the Trauma Symptom Inventory can track changes in Sarah's symptoms, functioning, and overall well-being over the course of therapy (Weathers et al., 2013; Briere, 1995). This ongoing evaluation allows her therapist to modify treatment approaches, redirect focus, or introduce additional interventions to ensure Sarah receives the most effective care.

Case Outcome:

Utilizing trauma-informed assessment tools and techniques, Sarah's therapist identifies her trauma-related symptoms accurately. This deepened understanding guides the development of an individualized treatment plan focusing on trauma-specific interventions. Over time, Sarah engages in therapies such as CPT and PE, which help her process her traumas, develop coping strategies, and improve her overall well-being. The trauma-informed approach not only assists in symptom reduction, but it also fosters empowerment, resilience, and post-traumatic growth in Sarah's life.

The significance of trauma-informed assessment tools and techniques in identifying trauma-related symptoms, improving treatment planning, and mitigating the risk of re-traumatization is evident in Sarah's case. These assessment tools provide insight into the profound impact of trauma on individuals' lives and inform the selection of appropriate interventions. By incorporating trauma-informed care principles and employing specialized assessment techniques, therapists can create a safe and supportive environment that promotes healing, reduces the risk of re-traumatization, and increases the likelihood of successful treatment outcomes for individuals who have experienced trauma.

4.5.2 *Implementation of Trauma-Informed Practices*

The implementation of trauma-informed practices is a critical aspect of providing effective supervision and treatment services for offending populations within correctional settings who have experienced trauma. Trauma-informed care focuses not only on treating the specific symptoms and consequences of trauma but also on creating a safe and supportive environment that promotes healing and resilience. The approach recognizes the widespread impact of trauma and acknowledges potential triggers and re-traumatization that can occur within the correctional setting. To successfully integrate trauma informed practices, staff within the correctional setting need appropriate training and education, as well as must engage in collaborative efforts and careful coordination of care.

4.5.2.1 Training and Education

Training and education initiatives focused on trauma-informed practices have several benefits within correctional settings. Firstly, they equip correctional staff with the skills and knowledge to recognize trauma symptoms, understand the impact of trauma on behaviors, and respond appropriately (Ford & Blaustein, 2013). This helps create an environment that avoids re-traumatization and promotes the healing and well-being of offending populations. Additionally, such initiatives can enhance staff resilience and job satisfaction, reducing burnout and turnover rates (Bloom & Covington, 2008).

Numerous research studies have demonstrated the positive outcomes of trauma-informed training and education for correctional staff. For example, research by Levenson & Willis (2019) found that correctional officers who received trauma-informed training reported improved relationships with offending populations, reduced use of disciplinary measures, and increased feelings of safety within the facility. Another study by Day et al. (2017) revealed that training led to improved staff attitudes, increased empathy, and enhanced communication skills when working with trauma survivors.

Successful implementation of trauma-informed practices among correctional staff requires several essential components. First, training should emphasize trauma awareness, providing a comprehensive understanding of trauma's impact and the principles of trauma-informed care (Levenson & Willis, 2019). It should also address the specific challenges faced by correctional staff working in a high-stress environment, to include de-escalation techniques and importance of self-care (Walker, 2021). Second, training should incorporate interactive methods, such as case studies, role-playing, and simulations, to enhance learning and promote skill application in real-life situations (Walker, 2021; Levenson & Willis, 2019). Lastly, ongoing support and supervision should be provided to maintain staff engagement and ensure the continued application of trauma-informed practices (Day et al., 2017). As such, training programs should be ongoing and incorporate feedback and evaluation to ensure continual professional development and competence in trauma informed care.

Overall, training and education initiatives focused on trauma-informed practices among correctional staff play a crucial role in supporting the rehabilitation and well-being of incarcerated individuals who have experienced trauma. With a comprehensive understanding of trauma and the skills to provide trauma-informed care, correctional staff can contribute to creating a safe and healing environment within correctional facilities. By implementing evidence-based training, incorporating interactive methods, and providing ongoing support, correctional facilities can foster a culture of empathy, reduce re-traumatization, and facilitate the successful reintegration of individuals into society.

4.5.2.2 Collaboration and Care Coordination

Collaboration and care coordination are foundational to trauma-informed care within correctional settings. By engaging key stakeholders, such as correctional officers, mental health professionals, medical staff, social workers, and administrators, in a shared decision-making process, it is possible to address the complex needs of trauma survivors effectively (Levensen & Willis, 2019). Collaboration ensures that trauma-informed principles are integrated into all aspects of correctional operations, thereby providing consistent support, reducing re-traumatization, and promoting positive outcomes (Forcada-Guex et al., 2006). Care coordination enables seamless communication and information sharing among providers (Segal et al., 2022), leading to a comprehensive understanding of offending populations'trauma histories, needs, and progress throughout their confinement.

Benefits of Collaboration and Care Coordination

Holistic Approaches: Collaboration allows for the integration of diverse perspectives, knowledge, and expertise to develop comprehensive treatment plans that address trauma-related issues alongside other mental health needs, substance abuse problems, and physical healthcare concerns (Kimberg & Wheeler, 2019).

Continuity of Care: Care coordination ensures that trauma-related care is coordinated during all phases of individuals' interactions with the correctional system, including pretrial, incarceration, and reentry. This promotes consistency, preventing fragmented care and increasing the chances of successful rehabilitation (Levenson & Willis, 2019).

Improved Communication: Collaboration fosters effective communication among staff members, creating an organizational culture that supports trauma-informed practices and helps maintain a safe and supportive environment for trauma survivors (Grella et al., 2000).

Reduced Staff Stress and Burnout: Collaborative efforts decrease the burden on individual staff members, enabling them to share responsibilities, enhance job satisfaction, and reduce stress and burnout (Levensen & Willis, 2019).

To foster collaboration and care coordination within a trauma-informed correctional setting, several strategies can be employed:

1. Interdisciplinary Training: Offer training programs that promote a shared understanding of trauma, its effects, and trauma-informed care principles for all staff members involved in the care of offending populations (Levenson & Willis, 2019).
2. Establish Communication Protocols: Develop guidelines for effective information sharing and communication among different departments and personnel involved in providing trauma-informed care (Segal et al., 2022).
3. Collaborative Case Conferences: Conduct regular meetings where various stakeholders come together to discuss individual cases, exchange information, and create comprehensive plans that integrate trauma-informed approaches (Kimberg & Wheeler 2019).
4. Supportive Policies and Resources: Implement policies that encourage and facilitate collaboration, provide access to necessary resources, and support trauma-informed practices in daily operations (Levensen & Willis, 2019).

As a result, collaboration and care coordination within a trauma-informed correctional setting is instrumental in promoting the rehabilitation and well-being of incarcerated individuals who have experienced trauma. By engaging stakeholders, ensuring holistic approaches, facilitating continuity of care, enhancing communication, and reducing staff stress, collaboration and care coordination lay the foundation for trauma-informed practices in correctional settings. Implementation of interdisciplinary training, communication protocols, collaborative case conferences, and supportive policies are essential strategies to achieve sustainable, trauma-informed correctional systems.

4.5.3 Fostering a Supportive and Empathetic Culture

Fostering a supportive and empathetic trauma-informed correctional setting is crucial for several reasons. Firstly, it acknowledges the experiences of incarcerated individuals who have suffered trauma, promoting an empathetic approach that respects their dignity and fosters healing (Levenson & Willis, 2019). Trauma-informed settings empower incarcerated individuals by providing opportunities for their voices to be heard, involving them in decision-making processes, and offering support that recognizes and addresses their specific trauma-related needs (McCuskey Shepley & Pasha, 2017).

Additionally, staff wellness and support play a vital role in creating a positive correctional environment. Providing staff members with resources, training, and support networks helps mitigate the negative effects of working in a high-stress environment, reducing burnout and turnover rates (Kimberg & Wheeler, 2019). When correctional staff feel valued and supported, they are better equipped to provide empathetic and effective care to incarcerated individuals, contributing to safer and more therapeutic interactions within the correctional setting (Kimberg & Wheeler, 2019).

Benefits of a Supportive and Empathetic Trauma-Informed Correctional Setting:

1. Enhanced Rehabilitation: A supportive and empathetic environment facilitates the healing and rehabilitation of incarcerated individuals who have experienced trauma. It provides opportunities for trauma-focused interventions, counseling, and support services that address the underlying causes of criminal behavior and contribute to better long-term outcomes (Miller & Najavits, 2012).
2. Increased Safety and Well-being: When trauma-informed practices are upheld, the correctional setting becomes safer for both staff and incarcerated individuals. Open communication, understanding, and empathy reduce the risk of re-traumatization, conflicts, and the use of punitive measures (Levenson et al., 2022).
3. Preventing Recidivism: By addressing the root causes of trauma and providing trauma-informed care, a supportive correctional environment can help break the cycle of reoffending. It equips individuals with the necessary skills, resources, and support networks for successful reintegration into society (Miller & Najavits, 2012).
4. Staff Satisfaction and Retention: When correctional staff's wellness and support are prioritized, job satisfaction and retention rates improve. This leads to a more experienced and committed workforce, fostering stability and consistency in trauma-informed care practices (Classen & Clark 2017).

A supportive and empathetic trauma-informed correctional setting that focuses both on the offending population and staff wellness and support, is essential for promoting rehabilitation, well-being, and positive outcomes. By recognizing the experiences of offending populations who have suffered trauma and providing them with opportunities to share their perspectives and participate in decision making processes, a trauma-informed correctional setting empowers them and promotes healing. Simultaneously, investing in staff wellness and support ensures a compassionate and competent workforce capable of providing effective and empathetic care. The benefits of such a correctional setting includes enhanced rehabilitation, increased safety, reduced recidivism rates, and improved staff satisfaction and retention. By fostering collaboration, communication, and shared commitment to trauma-informed practices, correctional settings can create environments that support the overall healing and well-being of both staff and offending populations, ultimately contributing to a more just and compassionate criminal justice system.

4.6 Conclusion

In conclusion, implementing trauma-informed approaches within the criminal justice system is crucial for addressing the needs of individuals who have experienced trauma and promoting their rehabilitation and well-being. This chapter has explored various aspects and components of trauma-informed care, highlighting the significance and benefits of adopting such approaches. Trauma-informed practices prioritize safety, trustworthiness, choice, collaboration, and empowerment, creating a supportive and healing environment for individuals involved in the criminal justice system. By recognizing the impact of trauma and understanding its far-reaching effects on individuals' behaviors and interactions, trauma-informed approaches shift the focus from punitive measures to understanding and addressing the underlying trauma that may contribute to criminal behavior.

Through trauma-informed assessment and screening processes, professionals in the criminal justice system can identify individuals who may have experienced trauma and tailor interventions accordingly. This includes providing trauma-specific interventions, such as trauma-focused therapy, that directly address the consequences of trauma and promote healing. Furthermore, collaboration and care coordination among various stakeholders within the criminal justice system are vital for successful implementation of trauma-informed approaches. Engaging correctional officers, mental health professionals, medical staff, social workers, administrators, and community organizations in a shared decision-making process contributes to a comprehensive and integrated approach to care.

The benefits of trauma-informed approaches in the criminal justice system are manifold. First and foremost, they promote better outcomes for individuals who have experienced trauma by addressing their unique needs in a safe and supportive environment. Trauma-informed practices also contribute to increased safety within correctional facilities, as they aim to reduce re-traumatization and the use of punitive measures, ultimately creating a more positive and therapeutic environment for both staff and inmates. Additionally, these approaches hold the potential to reduce recidivism rates by targeting the root causes of criminal behavior and providing individuals with the necessary tools and support for successful reintegration into society. When implemented effectively, trauma-informed practices can contribute to breaking the cycle of reoffending and promoting community safety.

It is important to note that the successful implementation and sustainability of trauma-informed approaches require ongoing training, resources, and support for all stakeholders involved. This includes continuous education for staff members, the development of trauma-informed policies and practices, and collaborative partnerships with community organizations to provide comprehensive care beyond the correctional facility.

In conclusion, trauma-informed approaches have the potential to transform the criminal justice system into a more compassionate, effective, and equitable system that prioritizes healing and well-being. By incorporating trauma-informed care principles into all aspects of the system, individuals who have experienced trauma can receive the support they need to move towards rehabilitation and a more positive future.

References

American Psychiatric Association. (2013). *Diagnostic and statistical manual of mental disorders* (5th ed.). American Psychiatric Publishing.

Bloom, B. E., & Covington, S. (2008). Addressing the mental health needs of women offenders. In *Women's mental health issues across the criminal justice system* (pp. 160–176).

Bloom, S. L. (2013). *Creating sanctuary: Toward the evolution of sane societies*. Routledge.

Briere, J. (1995). *Trauma Symptom Inventory (TSI)*. Professional Manual. Psychological Assessment Resources.

Briere, J. (1997). *Trauma Symptom Inventory (TSI)*. Professional Manual. Psychological Assessment Resources.

Briere, J., & Scott, C. (2012). *Principles of trauma therapy: A guide to symptoms, evaluation, and treatment*. Sage.

Briere, J., Scott, C., & Weathers, F. (2015). Peritraumatic and persistent dissociation in the presumed etiology of PTSD. *American Journal of Psychiatry, 172*(1), 12–20.

Chaudhri, S., Zweig, K. C., Hebbar, P., Angell, S., & Vasan, A. (2019). Trauma-informed care: a strategy to improve primary healthcare engagement for persons with criminal justice system involvement. *Journal of General Internal Medicine, 34*, 1048–1052.

Classen, C. C., & Clark, C. S. (2017). Trauma-informed care. In S. N. Gold (Ed.), *APA handbook of trauma psychology: Trauma practice* (pp. 515–541). American Psychological Association. https://doi.org/10.1037/0000020-025

Courtois, C. A., & Ford, J. D. (Eds.). (2009). *Treating complex traumatic stress disorders: An evidence-based guide* (p. 82). Guilford Press.

Day, A., Mohr, P., & Howells, K. (2017). Staff training in custodial agencies: An evaluation of an integrated model of training. *International Journal of Offender Therapy and Comparative Criminology, 61*(14), 1613–1637.

Drescher, J. (2018). Trauma-informed care for incarcerated persons: Progress and opportunities. *Psychological Services, 15*(4), 489–492.

Fallot, R. D., & Harris, M. (2008). Creating cultures of trauma-informed care (CCTIC): A self assessment and planning protocol. Community Connections.

Fazel, S., Hayes, A. J., Bartellas, K., Clerici, M., & Trestman, R. (2016). Mental health of prisoners: prevalence, adverse outcomes, and interventions. *The Lancet. Psychiatry, 3*(9), 871–881. https://doi.org/10.1016/S2215-0366(16)30142-0

Foa, E. B., Hembree, E. A., Rothbaum, B. O., & Rauch, S. (2007). *Prolonged exposure therapy for PTSD: Emotional processing of traumatic experiences: Therapist guide*. Oxford University Press.

Forcada-Guex, M., Pierrehumbert, B., Borghini, A., Moessinger, A., & Muller-Nix, C. (2006). Early dyadic patterns of mother–infant interactions and outcomes of prematurity at 18 months. *Pediatrics, 118*(1), e107–e114.

Ford, J. D., & Blaustein, M. E. (2013). Systemic self-regulation: A framework for trauma informed services in residential juvenile justice programs. *Journal of Family Violence, 28*(7), 665–677.

Ford, J. D., Grasso, D. J., Elhai, J. D., & Courtois, C. A. (2015). *Posttraumatic stress disorder: Scientific and professional dimensions*. Academic.

Ford, J. D., Chapman, J. F., Hawke, J., & Albert, D. (2007). *Trauma among youth in the juvenile justice system: Critical issues and new directions* (p. 6). National Center for Mental Health and Juvenile Justice.

Ford, J. D., Hartman, J. K., Hawke, J., & Chapman, J. F. (2010). Traumatic victimization, posttraumatic stress disorder, suicidal ideation, and substance abuse risk among juvenile justice-involved youth. *Journal of Child & Adolescent Trauma, 3*(3), 162–171.

Gould, R. A., Buckminster, S., Pollack, M. H., Otto, M. W., & Yap, L. (1997). Cognitive behavioral and pharmacological treatment for social phobia: a meta-analysis. *Clinical Psychology: Science and Practice, 4*(4), 291–306.

Green, B. L. (1996). Trauma History Questionnaire. In B. H. Stamm (Ed.), *Measurement of stress, trauma, and adaptation* (pp. 366–369). Sidran Press.

Grella, C. E., Joshi, V., & Hser, Y. I. (2000). Program variation in treatment outcomes among women in residential drug treatment. *Evaluation Review, 24*(4), 364–383.

Grella, C. E., Stein, J. A., & Greenwell, L. (2005). Associations among childhood trauma, adolescent problem behaviors, and adverse adult outcomes in substance-abusing women offenders. *Psychology of Addictive Behaviors, 19*(1), 43–53.

Harris, M., & Fallot, R. D. (2001). *Using trauma theory to design service systems*. Jersey-Bass.

Hobfoll, S. E., Hall, B. J., Canetti-Nisim, D., Galea, S., Johnson, R. J., & Palmieri, P. A. (2007). Refining our understanding of traumatic growth in the face of terrorism: Moving from meaning cognitions to doing what is meaningful. *Applied Psychology: An International Review, 56*(3), 345–366. https://doi.org/10.1111/j.1464-0597.2007.00292.x

Kilpatrick, D. G., Resnick, H. S., Milanak, M. E., Miller, M. W., Keyes, K. M., & Friedman, M. J. (2013). National estimates of exposure to traumatic events and PTSD prevalence using DSM-IV and DSM-5 criteria. *Journal of Traumatic Stress, 26*(5), 537–547.

Kessler, R. C., Sonnega, A., Bromet, E., Hughes, M., & Nelson, C. B. (2013). Posttraumatic stress disorder in the National Comorbidity Survey. In *Fear and anxiety* (pp. 22–34). Routledge.

Kimberg, L., & Wheeler, M. (2019). Trauma and trauma-informed care. In M. Gerber (Ed.), *Trauma-informed healthcare approaches*. Springer. https://doi.org/10.1007/978-3-030-04342-1_2

Levenson, J. S., & Willis, G. M. (2019). Implementing trauma-informed care in correctional treatment and supervision. *Journal of Aggression, Maltreatment & Trauma, 28*(4), 481–501.

Levenson, J. S., Prescott, D. S., & Willis, G. M. (2022). Trauma-informed treatment practices in criminal justice settings. In E. Jeglic & C. Calkins (Eds.), *Handbook of issues in criminal justice reform in the United States*. Springer. https://doi.org/10.1007/978-3-030-77565-0_24

McCuskey Shepley, M., & Pasha, S. (2017). *Design for mental and behavioral health* (1st ed.). Routledge. https://doi.org/10.4324/9781315646916

Mersky, J. P., Topitzes, J., & Reynolds, A. J. (2013). Impacts of adverse childhood experiences on health, mental health, and substance use in early adulthood: A cohort study of an urban, minority sample in the U.S. *Child Abuse & Neglect, 37*(11), 917–925.

Miller, N. A., & Najavits, L. M. (2012). Creating trauma-informed correctional care: A balance of goals and environment. *European Journal of Psychotraumatology, 3*, Article 17246. https://doi.org/10.3402/ejpt.v3i0.17246

Mills, K. L., Teesson, M., Ross, J., & Peters, L. (2006). Trauma, PTSD, and substance use disorders: Findings from the Australian National Survey of Mental Health and Well-Being. *American Journal of Psychiatry, 163*(4), 652–658.

Najavits, L. M. (2002). *Seeking safety: A treatment manual for PTSD and substance abuse*. Guilford Press.

Resick, P. A., Monson, C. M., & Chard, K. M. (2006). Cognitive processing therapy: Veteran/military version. *Clinical Psychology, 74*, 898–907.

Segal, M., Giuffrida, P., Possanza, L., & Bucciferro, D. (2022). The critical role of health information technology in the safe integration of behavioral health and primary care to improve patient care. *The Journal of Behavioral Health Services & Research, 49*(2), 221–230.

Scott, K. M., McLaughlin, K. A., Smith, D. A., & Ellis, P. M. (2012). Childhood maltreatment and DSM-IV adult mental disorders: Comparison of prospective and retrospective findings. *The British Journal of Psychiatry, 200*(6), 469–475.

Substance Abuse and Mental Health Services Administration. (2014). *SAMHSA's concept of Trauma and guidance for a trauma-informed approach* (No. (SMA) 14–4884). HHS Publication.

Van der Kolk, B. (2014). *The body keeps the score: Brain, mind, and body in the healing of trauma* (p. 3). Penguin Books.

Walker, T. (2021). Trauma-informed care in the criminal justice system. In D. A. Crighton & G. J. Towl (Eds.), *Forensic psychology*. https://doi.org/10.1002/9781394260669.ch35

Weathers, F. W., Litz, B. T., Keane, T. M., Palmieri, P. A., Marx, B. P., & Schnurr, P. P. (2013). *The ptsd checklist for dsm-5 (pcl-5)*. National Center for PTSD.

Weathers, F. W., Blake, D. D., Schnurr, P. P., Kaloupek, D. G., Marx, B. P., & Keane, T. M. (2018). *The Clinician-Administered PTSD Scale for DSM-5 (CAPS-5)*. National Center for PTSD.

Widom, C. S. (1989). The cycle of violence. *Science, 244*(4901), 160–166. https://doi.org/10.1126/science.2704995

Chapter 5
Breaking the Cycle: Interventions for Healing and Recovery Among Offenders with Developmental Trauma

Recidivism, or the tendency of a convicted criminal to reoffend, is a critical issue in the criminal justice system. Traditional approaches to punishment and rehabilitation have often failed to prevent the cycle of crime. In recent years, there has been a significant shift towards understanding the root causes of criminal behavior, with developmental trauma being identified as a key factor. This section examines the efficacy of trauma-informed interventions in reducing recidivism, analyzing various studies and research outcomes, while also considering the long-term benefits of addressing developmental trauma through the use of trauma-informed therapeutic approaches.

5.1 Trauma-Informed Interventions: A Framework for Healing

Trauma-informed care (TIC) is an approach that recognizes the presence of trauma in individuals and responds by integrating knowledge about trauma into practice (Abuse, 2014). It emphasizes physical, psychological, and emotional safety and helps survivors rebuild a sense of control over their lives (Harris & Fallot, 2001), while also standing at the intersection of psychological understanding and practical intervention, providing a framework where healing from trauma is not just an individual journey, but a systemic vision. Within the criminal justice system, this approach is employed to help individuals understand the impact of their trauma and develop coping strategies that discourage reoffending.

K. Sapp, *Exploring Developmental Trauma Disorder Among Offending Populations*, SpringerBriefs in Offending Populations & Correctional Psychotherapy, https://doi.org/10.1007/978-3-031-61157-5_5

5.1.1 *Impact on Recidivism*

Studies have shown that trauma-informed interventions can lead to a reduction in recidivism rates. Wolff and Shi (2010) found that within correctional facilities that implemented trauma-informed care, inmates were less likely to engage in misconducts, which often serve as precursors to reoffending after release. Similarly, it was noted that there have been studies that have demonstrated substantial improvements in behavioral health outcomes among women in a TIC program, suggesting a lower risk of recidivism upon reentry into society (Abuse, 2014).

The study conducted by Wolff and Shi (2010) provides an insightful analysis into the application and effectiveness of trauma-informed care within correctional settings. Optimizing the link between theoretical trauma awareness and practical implementation, the researchers focused their investigation on the impacts that trauma-informed interventions have on the behavior and well-being of incarcerated individuals. Their research is grounded in the recognition that a significant proportion of the prison population has experienced trauma at some point in their lives. Given that traditional correctional environments can inadvertently re-traumatize individuals, Wolff and Shi (2010) examined how a trauma-aware approach within the prison system could foster a safer and more supportive atmosphere, conducive to rehabilitation and less responsive to punitive triggers.

Wolff and Shi (2010) Key Findings

1. Reduction in Misconducts: The study revealed that trauma-informed training for correctional staff led to a noticeable decrease in inmate infractions. This is seen as reflective of an environment that is more attuned to the signs and symptoms of trauma and more skilled in de-escalating potentially volatile situations.
2. Staff Attitude and Culture Change: Correctional officers trained in TIC developed a more empathetic approach towards inmates, viewing them not just as offenders but as individuals with complex histories. This cultural shift potentially transforms the dynamics between staff and inmates, encouraging understanding over judgment.
3. Inmate Response: Inmates responded positively to a trauma-informed approach, displaying less aggression and more engagement with rehabilitative efforts. Recognizing the inmates' trauma backgrounds instilled a sense of safety and support, essential for behavior change and personal development.

The implications of their study suggest that trauma-informed corrections can contribute to a reduction in overall prison violence and tension, creating an environment that favors rehabilitation and potentially leading to lower recidivism upon release. Wolff and Shi's (2010) work, therefore, offers a valuable contribution to the discussion about how criminal justice systems can evolve to better meet the needs of incarcerated individuals, particularly those affected by trauma. Their study argues for a reexamination of how corrections facilities are structured and managed, with trauma-informed care at the cornerstone of this new model. However, it is important to note that the study by Wolff and Shi (2010) calls for further research into the long-term outcomes of the TIC approach in reducing recidivism, noting that the complexity of this field requires a multi-dimensional strategy that goes beyond initial findings.

5.1.2 The Long-Term Benefits of Addressing Developmental Trauma

Understanding and addressing developmental trauma is critical not only for the immediate well-being of affected individuals but also for their long-term mental and social health. Developmental trauma—trauma experienced during critical periods in early development—can have far-reaching impacts that last into adulthood, affecting an individual's ability to function and engage with society in healthy ways (van der Kolk, 2005). By addressing these traumas through therapies that focus on processing and healing, TIC interventions can pave the way towards healthier adulthood and contribute to the reduction of long-term adverse effects, including chronic health conditions, psychological disorders, and patterns that lead to increased interaction with the criminal justice system (Felitti et al., 1998).

TIC intervention in developmental trauma has been linked with decreased rates of recidivism, particularly in juvenile and criminal justice populations. When TIC therapeutic approaches are effectively employed to address underlying traumas, individuals are less likely to engage in repetitive criminal behavior (Ferencik & Ramirez-Hammond, 2019). This suggests that understanding and treating early trauma is not only a clinical issue but also a social and community safety priority. Addressing developmental trauma enhances emotional regulation and psychological resilience, leading to better coping strategies in stressful situations. This improved adaptability can be a buffer against behavioral issues and contribute to healthier social relationships (Cloitre, 2009). Over the long term, these skills can lead to greater educational attainment, stable employment, and reduced dependency on social services (Cicchetti & Rogosch, 1997).

5.1.2.1 Cost-Effectiveness of Trauma-Informed Approaches

Incarceration is a costly endeavor, and programs that reduce recidivism have the potential to deliver substantial cost savings. A report by Miller and Najavits (2012) indicated that trauma-informed therapies, by reducing the number of returning offenders, can alleviate the financial burden on the penal system. This aspect underscores the socio-economic benefits of TIC beyond its immediate psychological advantages.

Trauma-informed interventions have shown promise in reducing recidivism rates, leading to significant cost savings within the criminal justice system. Research by Lehrer (2021) found that addressing trauma among individuals involved in the justice system led to a decrease in criminal behaviors, resulting in lower rates of re-arrest and re-incarceration. This reduction in recidivism not only signifies improved public safety but also carries substantial financial benefits by reducing the strain on law enforcement, court systems, and correctional facilities (Lehrer, 2021).

Key Points to Consider

1. Reduction in Recidivism: Addressing trauma through trauma-informed approaches has been shown to reduce recidivism rates. By providing individuals with the necessary support and coping mechanisms to address trauma-related behaviors, these approaches can help prevent individuals from re-offending and returning to the criminal justice system. This reduction in recidivism translates to cost savings for the penal system, including reduced expenses related to incarceration, legal proceedings, and law enforcement efforts related to re-apprehension.
2. Improved Institutional Behavior: Within correctional facilities, trauma-informed approaches can lead to improvements in inmate behavior, reducing instances of violence, disciplinary infractions, and the need for heightened security measures. This can result in lower operational costs and a safer environment for both inmates and staff, decreasing the burden on the penal system.
3. Healthcare and Mental Health Cost Reduction: Unaddressed trauma often leads to mental health issues, substance abuse, and chronic health conditions among incarcerated individuals. By providing trauma-informed care and interventions, these issues can be addressed early on, potentially reducing the need for costly medical and mental health services within correctional facilities.
4. Enhanced Rehabilitation Outcomes: Trauma-informed approaches can contribute to more effective rehabilitation outcomes, preparing individuals for successful reintegration into society upon release. This can lead to reduced rates of recidivism, lower reliance on post-release support systems, and ultimately decreased strain on resources dedicated to post-release supervision and community re-entry programs.
5. Prevention of Violent Incidents and Staff Turnover: Addressing trauma among inmates can contribute to a safer and more stable institutional environment, leading to lower rates of violent incidents and staff turnover. This not only improves the overall well-being within correctional facilities but also reduces the financial and human resource costs associated with addressing and responding to security breaches and staff turnover.

(continued)

6. Potential for Economical Educational and Vocational Programs: Trauma-informed approaches can support the development of educational and vocational training programs within correctional facilities, facilitating inmates' reintegration into the workforce post-release. By effectively addressing trauma-related barriers to education and employment, these programs can contribute to reduced reliance on public assistance and increased economic productivity post-release.

Ultimately, trauma-informed approaches offer a comprehensive and proactive framework for addressing the complex needs of individuals within the penal system. By recognizing and responding to trauma, these approaches can mitigate the financial burden on the penal system, while also contributing to better long-term outcomes for inmates and society as a whole.

5.1.3 Conclusion

The adoption of trauma-informed interventions in reducing recidivism has shown promising results. Not only do these strategies appear to directly aid in reducing reoffending, but they also offer long-term benefits by addressing the developmental traumas that underlie criminal behaviors. As such, the continued integration of trauma-informed care within the criminal justice system has the potential to lead to more effective rehabilitation and a consequential reduction in recidivism. Further research and continued investment in TIC programs can maximize these outcomes, ultimately contributing to a safer and more just society.

5.2 Therapeutic Interventions for Developmental Trauma Among Offending Populations

The prevalence of developmental trauma among offending populations presents a significant challenge within the criminal justice system. Individuals with a history of developmental trauma often face a multitude of psychological and emotional difficulties, leading to maladaptive behaviors and involvement in criminal activities. Addressing this issue through trauma-informed interventions is crucial for breaking the cycle of reoffending and promoting long-term rehabilitation.

The significance of trauma-informed interventions lies in their ability to address the complex needs of individuals with developmental trauma within the context of the criminal justice system. Trauma-informed care emphasizes understanding the impact of trauma on an individual's life and delivering services in a manner that is sensitive and responsive to their trauma history (Harris & Fallot, 2001). By integrating trauma-informed approaches into rehabilitative programs, it is possible to provide tailored support that recognizes the underlying trauma experienced by offending populations.

Another key significance of trauma-informed interventions is their potential to prevent retraumatization of individuals within the justice system. Traditional approaches within the criminal justice system often overlook the impact of trauma, leading to situations where individuals with developmental trauma may be retraumatized through punitive measures or lack of understanding (Bath, 2008). Trauma-informed interventions seek to create a safe and supportive environment that minimizes the risk of retraumatization and promotes a sense of empowerment and resilience among individuals with developmental trauma.

Trauma-informed interventions play a crucial role in promoting healing and recovery among individuals with developmental trauma. By utilizing evidence-based therapies such as trauma-focused cognitive behavioral therapy (TF-CBT) and Eye Movement Desensitization and Reprocessing (EMDR), it is possible to address the underlying trauma symptoms and promote adaptive coping mechanisms (Cohen et al., 2016). These interventions not only reduce trauma-related symptoms but also contribute to improving overall mental health outcomes and reducing the risk of reoffending among individuals within the justice system (Ford et al., 2006).

5.2.1 Trauma-Focused Cognitive Behavioral Therapy (TF-CBT)

Trauma-Focused Cognitive Behavioral Therapy (TF-CBT) has emerged as an evidenced-based intervention for addressing trauma related symptoms among various populations, including offenders with a history of developmental trauma. As a structured, evidence-based therapy designed to help individuals, including children and adolescents, overcome the negative effects of trauma, TF-CBT incorporates cognitive-behavioral techniques and trauma-specific interventions to address distorted beliefs and negative emotions resulting from trauma exposure (Cohen et al., 2016).

One notable study by Cohen et al. (2004) conducted a randomized controlled trial to evaluate the effectiveness of TF-CBT among juvenile offenders with a history of developmental trauma. In their randomized controlled trial, Cohen et al. (2004) investigated the effectiveness of TF-CBT in reducing trauma symptoms and improving functioning among a sample of juvenile offenders with a history of developmental trauma. The study included a control group and a treatment group that received TF-CBT, and participants were assessed before and after the intervention. The results revealed significant improvements in post-traumatic stress symptoms and overall adaptive functioning among the treatment group compared to the control group (Cohen et al., 2004).

The findings of the study by Cohen et al. (2004) hold significant implications for the utilization of TF-CBT within the criminal justice system. The demonstrated effectiveness of TF-CBT in reducing trauma symptoms and improving functioning among juvenile offenders with developmental trauma highlights the potential for integrating this evidence-based intervention into rehabilitative programs. By incorporating TF-CBT into the treatment framework for individuals within the justice system, it is possible to address the underlying trauma symptoms and contribute to long-term rehabilitation and reintegration.

Furthermore, the study by Cohen et al. (2004) emphasizes the importance of providing trauma-informed care within the criminal justice system. By offering evidence-based interventions such as TF-CBT, it is possible to create a supportive and tailored approach that recognizes the complex needs of individuals with developmental trauma. This not only promotes healing and recovery but also reduces the risk of reoffending and contributes to the overall well-being of individuals impacted by trauma within the justice system.

In conclusion, the randomized controlled trial conducted by Cohen et al. (2004) provides compelling evidence for the effectiveness of TF-CBT in addressing developmental trauma among juvenile offenders. The study's findings underscore the potential impact of TF-CBT within the criminal justice system, highlighting the need for incorporating evidence-based trauma-focused interventions into rehabilitative programs. By utilizing TF-CBT, the justice system can play a pivotal role in breaking the cycle of reoffending and promoting long-term rehabilitation and recovery for individuals impacted by developmental trauma.

5.2.2 Eye Movement Desensitization and Reprocessing (EMDR)

EMDR is another trauma-focused intervention that has gained recognition for its effectiveness in treating trauma-related symptoms. This therapy involves standardized protocols that include phases such as desensitization, installation of positive cognition, and closure (Shapiro, 2017). A meta-analysis by Chen et al. (2014) examined the effectiveness of EMDR in children and adolescents with post-traumatic stress disorder (PTSD) and found significant reductions in trauma-related symptoms, indicating the potential of EMDR in addressing developmental trauma among at-risk youth within the justice system.

The meta-analysis by Chen et al. (2014) holds important implications for the utilization of EMDR within the criminal justice system. The demonstrated effectiveness of EMDR in reducing trauma-related symptoms among children and adolescents with PTSD suggests the potential for integrating this trauma-focused intervention into rehabilitative programs for at-risk youth involved in the justice system. By incorporating EMDR, it is possible to address the impact of developmental trauma and promote healing and recovery in a population that is particularly vulnerable to the long-term effects of trauma.

Furthermore, the findings of the meta-analysis underscore the importance of offering evidence-based trauma-focused interventions within the criminal justice system. By integrating EMDR into the treatment paradigm for at-risk youth, it is possible to provide tailored support that recognizes the unique trauma experiences of individuals within this population. This not only contributes to reducing trauma-related symptoms but also fosters a sense of resilience and promotes long-term rehabilitation and reintegration.

In conclusion, the meta-analysis conducted by Chen et al. (2014) provides compelling evidence for the effectiveness of EMDR in addressing developmental trauma among at-risk youth, including those within the criminal justice system. The meta-analysis's findings highlight the potential impact of EMDR within rehabilitative programs, underscoring the need for evidence-based trauma-focused interventions tailored to the unique needs of at-risk youth. By utilizing EMDR, the justice system can play a critical role in fostering healing and recovery, ultimately contributing to the long-term well-being of individuals impacted by developmental trauma within the justice system.

5.2.3 Other Evidence-Based Therapies

In addition to TF-CBT and EMDR, other evidence-based therapies have shown promise in addressing developmental trauma among offending populations. For instance, Trauma Systems Therapy (TST) emphasizes the need for comprehensive and multi-systemic interventions to address trauma-related symptoms and improve functioning among at-risk youth (Saxe et al., 2007). Research by Saxe et al. (2007) demonstrated the effectiveness of TST in improving mental health outcomes and reducing delinquent behaviors among traumatized youth within the justice system, shedding light on the potential of this approach in addressing developmental trauma.

Dialectical Behavior Therapy (DBT) has also demonstrated relevance in addressing developmental trauma among offending populations. DBT emphasizes the development of emotion regulation skills, distress tolerance, and interpersonal effectiveness, which are particularly beneficial for individuals with a history of trauma. Research has shown that DBT can reduce self-harming behavior and improve emotional regulation among individuals with complex trauma histories (Harned et al., 2014).

Mindfulness-based interventions have also shown promise in addressing developmental trauma among offending populations. Mindfulness practices can enhance emotion regulation and reduce reactivity to trauma triggers, promoting greater self-awareness and coping skills. Research has indicated that mindfulness-based interventions can reduce symptoms of PTSD and improve overall well-being among individuals with trauma histories, including those within the justice system (Boyd et al., 2018).

Internal Family Systems Therapy (IFS) has been recognized for its efficacy in addressing complex trauma presentations. IFS focuses on understanding and integrating various parts of a person's internal system, recognizing the impact of trauma on these internal dynamics. Research has shown that IFS can lead to significant improvements in symptom reduction and interpersonal functioning among individuals with complex trauma histories, including those involved in the justice system (Gantt & Tinnin, 2007).

In conclusion, several evidenced-based therapies have shown promise in addressing developmental trauma among offending populations. Trauma Systems Therapy (TST), Dialectical Behavior Therapy (DBT), mindfulness-based interventions, and Internal Family Systems Therapy (IFS) all offer tailored approaches that recognize the unique needs of individuals with developmental trauma within the justice system. By integrating these evidence-based therapies into rehabilitative programs, the justice system can play a crucial role in fostering healing, promoting recovery, and reducing the risk of reoffending among individuals impacted by developmental trauma.

5.2.3.1 Trauma Systems Therapy (TST)

Trauma Systems Therapy (TST) has emerged as a comprehensive, multi-systemic intervention for addressing trauma-related symptoms among youth exposed to complex trauma. Saxe et al. (2007) conducted a seminal study to evaluate the effectiveness of TST in improving the mental health outcomes for youth with complex trauma histories. The research encompassed an examination of the impact of TST on trauma-related symptoms, functional impairment, and overall well-being among a diverse sample of youth, including those with justice involvement. The results revealed significant improvements in mental health outcomes, as evidenced by reductions in trauma symptoms and functional impairment, alongside improved adaptive functioning in various domains (Saxe et al., 2007).

The findings of the study by Saxe et al. (2007) carry critical implications for the integration of Trauma Systems Therapy within the criminal justice system. The demonstrated effectiveness of TST in improving mental health outcomes, reducing trauma symptoms, and enhancing adaptive functioning underscores the value of incorporating this multi-systemic intervention into rehabilitative programs for offending youth. By integrating TST, the justice system can address the complex trauma experiences of youth within its care, providing a holistic and trauma-informed approach to promote healing and recovery.

Furthermore, Saxe et al. (2007) emphasize how Trauma Systems Therapy acknowledges the complex needs of youth with trauma histories and aims to modify the broader systems surrounding these individuals. By implementing TST within the justice system, stakeholders can address the intricate interplay between individual trauma symptoms, family dynamics, peer relationships, and community influences, ultimately promoting long-term healing and resilience among youth impacted by developmental trauma.

In conclusion, the research conducted by Saxe et al. (2007) provides robust evidence for the effectiveness of Trauma Systems Therapy in improving mental health outcomes for youth with complex trauma histories, including those within the justice system. The study's findings underline the potential impact of TST within rehabilitative programs, highlighting the need for trauma-informed, multi-systemic interventions that address the comprehensive needs of youth impacted by developmental trauma. By utilizing Trauma Systems Therapy, the criminal justice system can play a pivotal role in fostering healing, promoting recovery, and reducing the long-term impact of developmental trauma among offending youth.

5.2.3.1.1 Adapting Trauma Systems Therapy for Adult Offending Populations

Trauma Systems Therapy (TST) has demonstrated effectiveness in addressing trauma-related symptoms among youth with complex trauma histories. The core principles of TST, which emphasize a multi-systemic, comprehensive approach to addressing trauma, can be adapted to meet the needs of adult offending populations. The foundational components of TST, such as the focus on enhancing support networks, addressing individual trauma symptoms within the context of broader systems, and promoting resilience, can be tailored to the experiences and challenges faced by adult offenders (Saxe et al., 2007). The adaptation of Trauma Systems Therapy for adult offending populations holds significant implications for the criminal justice system. By integrating trauma-informed, multisystemic interventions tailored to the unique developmental trajectories and needs of adult offenders, the justice system can foster a more comprehensive approach to rehabilitation and reintegration. Addressing trauma within the context of adult offending demands a nuanced understanding of the intersecting systems influencing individual well-being, including carceral environments, community support networks, and ongoing stressors post-release (Dvoskin & Heilbrun, 2001).

One key adaptation involves recognizing the long-term impact of developmental trauma on adults within the justice system. TST can be modified to address the cumulative effects of trauma across the lifespan, integrating interventions that acknowledge the complex interplay between childhood trauma, ongoing stressors, and the unique trauma experiences encountered within carceral settings (Ford et al., 2011). Furthermore, adapting Trauma Systems Therapy for adult offenders involves a shift in focus towards addressing the pervasive impact of trauma on various domains, such as interpersonal relationships, coping strategies, and community reintegration. Tailoring TST interventions to address the systemic challenges faced by adult offenders, including re-entry into society and the complexities of navigating post-release support systems, is crucial for promoting long-term healing and reducing the risk of recidivism (Green et al., 2016).

Utilizing an adapted version of TST within the criminal justice system underscores the importance of recognizing the prolonged impact of trauma on adult offenders. By addressing the systemic challenges and trauma-related symptoms that underpin offending behavior, stakeholders can play a critical role in promoting healing, reducing recidivism, and supporting long-term well-being among this often-overlooked population. As such, adapting Trauma Systems Therapy for adult offending populations offers the potential to address developmental trauma within the criminal justice system comprehensively. By tailoring the core principles of TST to meet the specific needs of adult offenders, stakeholders can promote healing, reduce recidivism, and foster long-term well-being. The adaptation of TST provides an opportunity to reconceptualize the rehabilitative approach within the context of the justice system, recognizing the enduring impact of trauma and the potential for comprehensive, trauma-informed interventions to support long-term recovery among adult offenders.

5.2.3.2 Dialectical Behavior Therapy (DBT)

Dialectical Behavior Therapy (DBT) has shown promise as an effective intervention for addressing developmental trauma among adult offending populations within the criminal justice system. The foundations of DBT, developed by Marsha Linehan, align well with the multifaceted needs of this population. DBT integrates a range of strategies, including mindfulness, emotion regulation, distress tolerance, and interpersonal effectiveness, tailored to address the specific difficulties associated with developmental trauma and offending behavior. For adults with trauma histories, DBT's emphasis on emotion regulation and distress tolerance can provide crucial skills for managing overwhelming emotions and reducing impulsive and risky behaviors often associated with offending.

Furthermore, the integration of mindfulness practices within DBT can support adult offenders in developing present-moment awareness, reducing reactivity, and fostering non-judgmental acceptance—all of which are pertinent to addressing the impact of developmental trauma. By cultivating mindfulness skills, individuals can gradually learn to regulate intense emotions, manage triggers associated with trauma, and bolster their capacity to make more adaptive choices, thereby reducing the likelihood of reoffending. The comprehensive nature of DBT, with its combination of individual therapy, skills training, phone coaching, and therapist consultation, allows for a more layered and adaptive approach, ultimately supporting the unique needs of adult offenders with developmental trauma. These individuals often require a multifaceted and flexible intervention that addresses cognitive, emotional, and behavioral challenges, and DBT provides this level of comprehensive support.

Empirical evidence supporting the applicability of DBT for trauma-related symptoms and impulsive behaviors further underscores its potential utility in this context. Research has demonstrated the effectiveness of DBT in reducing suicide attempts, self-harm behaviors, and symptoms of post-traumatic stress disorder (PTSD) among individuals with complex trauma histories, suggesting its potential to similarly impact adult offenders with developmental trauma (Harned et al., 2014).

Implementing DBT within correctional settings necessitates a systematic and tailored approach, incorporating training for staff, ongoing supervision, and integration with existing rehabilitative programs. By integrating DBT into the treatment framework for adult offenders with developmental trauma, the criminal justice system can offer a more comprehensive and responsive approach to addressing the deeply ingrained effects of trauma, promoting healing, reducing recidivism, and supporting long-term well-being.

Dialectical Behavior Therapy presents a viable intervention for developmental trauma among adult offending populations. With its tailored focus on emotion regulation, distress tolerance, and mindfulness, DBT provides a comprehensive and adaptable approach that can effectively address the complexities of trauma-related symptoms and offending behavior. By integrating DBT into the treatment continuum within the criminal justice system, it offers promise in promoting long-term healing and rehabilitation for this population.

5.2.3.3 Mindfulness-Based Interventions

Mindfulness-based interventions offer a promising avenue for addressing the complex impact of developmental trauma among adult offenders. These interventions, including Mindfulness-Based Stress Reduction (MBSR) and Mindfulness-Based Cognitive Therapy (MBCT), emphasize present-moment awareness, non-judgmental acceptance, and compassionate self-regulation. Research indicates that mindfulness practice promotes neural changes, emotional regulation, and enhanced coping strategies, all of which are pertinent to addressing the effects of developmental trauma (Kuyken et al., 2008). Empirical evidence supports the efficacy of mindfulness-based interventions in reducing symptoms of depression, anxiety, and post-traumatic stress disorder (PTSD) among various populations, demonstrating the potential for similar benefits among adult offenders with developmental trauma (Boyd et al., 2018). Furthermore, mindfulness training has been shown to enhance emotional regulation, reduce aggression, and improve impulse control, all of which are pertinent to addressing offending behavior associated with developmental trauma (Sharma & Rush, 2014).

The integration of mindfulness-based interventions within the criminal justice system holds significant implications for promoting healing and reducing recidivism among adult offenders with developmental trauma. By incorporating mindfulness practices into rehabilitative programs and post-release support, the justice system can offer a comprehensive approach to addressing the enduring impact of developmental trauma, promoting long-term well-being and community reintegration (Bowen et al., 2009). By emphasizing mindfulness-based interventions, the criminal justice system can foster a trauma-informed approach that recognizes the chronic effects of developmental trauma and offers evidence-based interventions to promote healing and recovery. Mindfulness training provides adult offenders with the tools to cultivate self-awareness, emotional regulation, and prosocial behaviors, ultimately reducing the likelihood of recidivism and promoting long-term well-being (Bowen et al., 2009).

Ultimately, mindfulness-based interventions offer a promising avenue for addressing developmental trauma among adult offending populations. The evidence supporting the effectiveness of mindfulness practices in enhancing emotional regulation, reducing symptoms of psychological distress, and promoting prosocial behaviors underscores the potential for mindfulness-based interventions to mitigate the impact of developmental trauma. By integrating mindfulness into rehabilitative programs, the criminal justice system can play a pivotal role in fostering healing, reducing recidivism, and supporting long-term well-being for adult offenders impacted by developmental trauma.

5.2.3.4 Internal Family Systems Therapy (IFS)

The Internal Family Systems model, developed by Richard Schwartz, proposes that individuals have distinct parts within them that carry different emotions, beliefs, and intentions. These parts are organized into an internal system, and the model aims to help individuals navigate and integrate these parts through a process of self-discovery and self-leadership. In the context of adult offenders with developmental trauma, the IFS approach provides a framework for understanding and engaging with the various fragmented aspects of their internal experiences. It recognizes that many adult offenders have adaptive parts that emerged as a response to traumatic experiences, and these parts often manifest as maladaptive coping mechanisms, such as aggression, substance abuse, or self-sabotage.

By using IFS, therapists can help adult offenders explore and understand these fragmented parts, provide space for these parts to be witnessed and heard, and ultimately facilitate integration and healing. This approach can lead to reduced impulsivity, improved emotional regulation, and a greater sense of self-compassion, thereby mitigating the impact of developmental trauma and reducing the risk of reoffending. There is growing empirical support for the effectiveness of IFS in addressing trauma-related symptoms, both in clinical and non-clinical populations. Studies have highlighted its potential in reducing PTSD symptoms, improving emotional regulation, and promoting self-compassion, which are critical factors in addressing the impact of developmental trauma among adult offenders (Gantt & Tinnin, 2007).

Implementing IFS within correctional settings for adult offenders with developmental trauma requires a comprehensive and well-trained approach. Integrating this model into therapy programs can provide adult offenders with a deeper understanding of their internal experiences, fostering empathy for themselves and others, and ultimately helping them develop healthier coping strategies. Additionally, it enables them to address the root causes of their offending behavior, paving the way for a more successful rehabilitation and reintegration process.

In conclusion, the Internal Family Systems model offers a promising intervention for developmental trauma among adult offending populations. By recognizing and engaging with the fragmented parts of individuals' internal experiences, IFS can effectively address the deep-rooted impact of trauma, ultimately promoting healing, reducing recidivism, and supporting long-term well-being among this demographic.

5.2.4 Conclusion

In conclusion, trauma-informed interventions, such as TF-CBT, EMDR, and other evidence-based therapies, hold promise in addressing developmental trauma among offending populations. These interventions have demonstrated effectiveness in reducing trauma symptoms, improving mental health outcomes, and contributing to the overall rehabilitation of individuals within the criminal justice system. By incorporating these trauma-focused approaches into rehabilitative programs, it is possible to break the cycle of reoffending and promote long-term healing and recovery for those impacted by developmental trauma.

5.3 Conclusion

In conclusion, the importance of trauma-informed interventions in addressing developmental trauma among offending populations cannot be overstated. By integrating trauma-informed care into the criminal justice system, it is possible to provide tailored support that recognizes the complex needs of individuals with developmental trauma, promotes healing and recovery, and prevents retraumatization. Through the implementation of trauma-informed approaches, the criminal justice system can contribute to breaking the cycle of reoffending and fostering long-term rehabilitation for those impacted by developmental trauma.

References

Abuse, S. (2014). *Trauma-informed care in behavioral health services.* (No Title), 42.

Bath, H. (2008). The three pillars of trauma-informed care. *Reclaiming Children and Youth, 17*(3), 17–21.

Bowen, S., Chawla, N., Collins, S. E., Witkiewitz, K., Hsu, S., Grow, J., Clifasefi, S., Garner, M., Douglass, A., Larimer, M., & Marlatt, A. (2009). Mindfulness-based relapse prevention for substance use disorders: A pilot efficacy trial. *Substance Abuse, 30*(4), 295–305.

Boyd, J. E., Lanius, R. A., & McKinnon, M. C. (2018). Mindfulness-based treatments for posttraumatic stress disorder: A review of the treatment literature and neurobiological evidence. *Journal of Psychiatry & Neuroscience, 43*(1), 7–25. https://doi.org/10.1503/jpn.170021

Chen, Y.-R., Hung, K.-W., Tsai, J.-C., Chu, H., Chung, M.-H., et al. (2014). Efficacy of eye-movement desensitization and reprocessing for patients with posttraumatic-stress disorder: A meta-analysis of randomized controlled trials. *PLoS One, 9*(8), e103676. https://doi.org/10.1371/journal.pone.0103676

Cicchetti, D., & Rogosch, F. A. (1997). The role of self-organization in the promotion of resilience in maltreated children. *Development and Psychopathology, 9*(4), 797–815.

Cloitre, M. (2009). Effective psychotherapies for posttraumatic stress disorder: A review and critique. *CNS Spectrums, 14*(1), 32–43.

Cohen, J. A., Deblinger, E., Mannarino, A. P., & Steer, R. A. (2004). A multisite, randomized controlled trial for children with sexual abuse–related PTSD symptoms. *Journal of the American Academy of Child & Adolescent Psychiatry, 43*(4), 393–402.

Cohen, J. A., Mannarino, A. P., & Deblinger, E. (2016). *Treating trauma and traumatic grief in children and adolescents* (2nd ed.). Guilford Press.

Dvoskin, J. A., & Heilbrun, K. (2001). Risk assessment and release decision-making: Toward resolving the great debate. *Journal-American Academy of Psychiatry and the Law, 29*, 6–10.

Felitti, V. J., Anda, R. F., Nordenberg, D., Williamson, D. F., Spitz, A. M., Edwards, V., & Marks, J. S. (1998). Relationship of childhood abuse and household dysfunction to many of the leading causes of death in adults: The Adverse Childhood Experiences (ACE) Study. *American Journal of Preventive Medicine, 14*(4), 245–258.

Ferencik, S. D., & Ramirez-Hammond, R. (2019). *Trauma-informed care: Best practices and protocols for Ohio's domestic violence programs*. Ohio Domestic Violence Network.

Ford, J. D., Chapman, J., Mack, J. M., & Pearson, G. (2006). Pathways from traumatic child victimization to delinquency: Implications for juvenile and permanency court proceedings and decisions. *Juvenile and Family Court Journal, 57*, 13–26. https://doi.org/10.1111/j.1755-6988.2006.tb00111.x

Ford, J. D., Wasser, T., & Connor, D. F. (2011). Identifying and determining the symptom severity associated with polyvictimization among psychiatrically impaired children in the outpatient setting. *Child Maltreatment, 16*(3), 216–226.

Gantt, L., & Tinnin, L. W. (2007). Intensive trauma therapy of PTSD and dissociation: An outcome study. *The Arts in Psychotherapy, 34*(1), 69–80. https://doi.org/10.1016/j.aip.2006.09.007

Green, B. L., Saunders, P. A., Power, E., Dass-Brailsford, P., Schelbert, K. B., Giller, E., & Wani, A. (2016). Trauma-informed medical care: Patient response to a primary care provider communication training program. *Journal of Loss and Trauma, 21*(2), 147–159.

Harned, M. S., Korslund, K. E., & Linehan, M. M. (2014). A pilot randomized controlled trial of dialectical behavior therapy with and without the dialectical behavior therapy prolonged exposure protocol for suicidal and self-injuring women with borderline personality disorder and PTSD. *Behaviour Research and Therapy, 55*, 7–17.

Harris, M., & Fallot, R. D. (2001). *Using trauma theory to design service systems*. Jossey-Bass.

Kolk, B. A. V. D. (2005). Developmental Trauma Disorder-A more specific diagnosis than post-traumatic stress disorder should be considered for children with complex trauma histories. *Psychiatric Annals, 35*(5), 401–409.

Kuyken, W., Byford, S., Taylor, R. S., Watkins, E., Holden, E., White, K., Barrett, B., Byng, R., Evans, A., Mullan, E., & Teasdale, J. D. (2008). Mindfulness-based cognitive therapy to prevent relapse in recurrent depression. *Journal of Consulting and Clinical Psychology, 78*(3), 275–286.

Lehrer D. (2021). Trauma-Informed Care: The Importance of Understanding the Incarcerated Women. *Journal of Correctional Health Care: The Official Journal of the National Commission on Correctional Health Care, 27*(2), 121–126. https://doi.org/10.1089/jchc.20.07.0060

Miller, N. A., & Najavits, L. M. (2012). Creating trauma-informed correctional care: A balance of goals and environment. *European Journal of Psychotraumatology, 3*(1), 17246.

Saxe, G. N., Ellis, B. H., & Kaplow, J. B. (2007). *Collaborative treatment of traumatized children and teens: The trauma systems therapy approach*. Guilford Press.

Shapiro, F. (2017). *Eye movement desensitization and reprocessing therapy: Basic principles, protocols, and procedures*. Guilford Press.

Sharma, M., & Rush, S. E. (2014). Mindfulness-based stress reduction as a stress management intervention for healthy individuals: A systematic review. *Journal of Evidence-Based Complementary & Alternative Medicine, 19*(4), 271–286.

Wolff, N. L., & Shi, J. (2010). Trauma and incarcerated persons. In C. L. Scott (Ed.), Handbook of correctional mental health (2., pp. 277–320). American Psychiatric Publishing, Inc..

Chapter 6
Policy Implications and Recommendations

6.1 Current Shortcomings in the Criminal Justice System

Experiences of developmental trauma—severe adversities in childhood affecting an individual's development—have been strongly linked to a heightened risk of engaging in criminal behavior (DeLisi et al., 2017). Despite this evidence, the criminal justice system has been slow to systematically integrate this knowledge into its practices. Understanding how the system currently fails to account for developmental trauma is pivotal in proposing reforms capable of effectively rehabilitative and reintegrative outcomes.

The criminal justice system, which encompasses a broad swath from law enforcement to correctional institutions, has traditionally maintained a primary focus on the deterrence, punishment, and containment of criminal behavior. Despite its pivotal role in societal safety and justice, the system is consistently criticized for its limited success in addressing the underlying causes that contribute to criminal behavior, including developmental trauma (DeLisi et al., 2017).

Below are some detailed shortcomings concerning developmental trauma within the criminal justice system:

1. Neglect of Developmental Trauma in Assessments and Interventions
   Although awareness about the impact of early trauma on later behaviors is mounting, this knowledge has not been fully integrated into the procedures or the ethos of the criminal justice system. Offenders are often processed through the system without thorough assessments for developmental trauma, which is crucial for tailoring interventions that address the roots of their criminal behavior (Bonta & Andrews, 2016). For example, Miller and Najavits (2012) argued that criminal justice settings frequently lack the protocols to identify individuals affected by trauma, thereby missing critical opportunities for intervention and support.

K. Sapp, *Exploring Developmental Trauma Disorder Among Offending Populations*, SpringerBriefs in Offending Populations & Correctional Psychotherapy, https://doi.org/10.1007/978-3-031-61157-5_6

2. Systemic Resistance to Rehabilitative Models
   The persistent belief in retributive justice over rehabilitative models has fostered a system that prioritizes punishment over recovery or behavioral change. This pervasive philosophy is evident in stringent policies that emphasize incarceration over community-based rehabilitation, which could be more beneficial for those affected by developmental trauma. The result is a rigid system where transformative opportunities are lost, and the cycle of crime remains unbroken (DeLisi et al., 2017).
   The role of the criminal justice system transcends the mere adjudication of guilt; it encompasses the manifold responsibility of deterrence, rehabilitation, and public safety. Despite this, there is a stark inadequacy in the system's ability to rehabilitate, especially regarding individuals with developmental trauma—a shortcoming deeply rooted in a systemic resistance to rehabilitative models.

The resistance to rehabilitative models takes shape through a range of systemic structures and practices:

- Retributive Justice Over Restorative Approaches
  Historically, the criminal justice system has favored a retributive model of justice—one that prioritizes punishment over restoration or healing. Of particular concern is the management of offenders who have experienced developmental trauma. This preference for punishment is evident in the policies that favor incarceration and harsh penalties over therapeutic or community-based rehabilitative strategies that could potentially address the underlying trauma contributing to criminal behaviors (Clear et al., 2018).
- Policy and Legislative Challenges
  Policies, such as mandatory minimum sentences and 'three strikes' laws, exacerbate this resistance to rehabilitative models by limiting the discretion of judges and emphasizing a one-size-fits-all approach to sentencing. Such policies can disproportionately affect those with developmental trauma by ignoring individual circumstances and the potential for rehabilitation (Simon, 2020).
- Fiscal Prioritization and Resources Allocation
  There is a notable lack of investment in rehabilitative programs within the corrections system. The fiscal priorities of many correctional systems are skewed towards maintaining and building facilities over funding rehabilitation programs or training for correctional staff in trauma-informed approaches (Chen & Shapiro, 2007).
- Correctional Environment and Culture
  The nature of correctional institutions often runs counter to the needs of those with developmental trauma. Facilities frequently prioritize control and security over rehabilitation, creating environments that are themselves traumatizing and counter-therapeutic. This is compounded by a correctional culture that often stigmatizes mental health issues and values toughness over vulnerability (Miller & Najavits, 2012).

- Ineffective Training and Education
  Even within a punitive system, professionals who recognize the value of rehabilitation face a lack of effective training in implementing such models. Without appropriate education regarding developmental trauma and its effects, criminal justice professionals, including police, attorneys, judges, and correctional officers, are likely to perpetuate a punitive approach, even inadvertently (Abuse, 2014).
- Evidence-Based Practices (EBPs) Implementation
  While there is a growing body of research demonstrating the effectiveness of EBPs in addressing developmental trauma within the offender population, these practices are not widely implemented due to skepticism, resistance to change, and lack of knowledge at various levels of the criminal justice system (Staton & Lurigio, 2016).

Overcoming systemic resistance to rehabilitative models requires acknowledging that offenders with histories of developmental trauma may continue to cycle through the criminal justice system if not appropriately addressed. Transformative change will demand intentional shifts in policy, culture, resources, and training to prioritize humanizing and restorative justice approaches that honor individual histories and promote rehabilitation (Mathiesen, 2014). Addressing the needs of those with developmental trauma within the criminal justice system not only aligns with moral imperatives of care and social justice but holds promise for reducing recidivism, enhancing public safety, and creating healthier communities.

3. Insufficient Staff Training and Resources
   Law enforcement officers, judicial staff, and correctional officers frequently lack the training needed to understand, recognize, and appropriately respond to signs of developmental trauma in the populations they serve (Abuse, 2014). Without this knowledge, they are ill-equipped to interact in a trauma-informed manner, which can exacerbate the trauma symptoms in individuals and negatively affect rehabilitation efforts.

4. Lack of Trauma-Informed Practices
   The criminal justice system has been slow to adopt trauma-informed care as a standard practice. A trauma-informed approach necessitates changes at multiple levels, including policy modification, environment adaptation, and interagency collaboration, to create a holistic and supportive system for trauma survivors (Harris & Fallot, 2001). The absence of such comprehensive practices can perpetuate harm and stymie successful rehabilitation and reintegration of offenders (Miller & Najavits, 2012).

5. Fragmentation of Services
   The fragmentation of services is a critical shortcoming within the criminal justice system that impedes the effective recognition and treatment of developmental trauma among offending populations. The disconnection between mental health services, child protective services, and criminal justice entities, that interact with

offending populations with a history of trauma which results in piecemeal care and missed opportunities for comprehensive treatment (Harris & Fallot, 2001).

More specifically, it represents a systemic flaw that hinders rehabilitative efforts and contributes to poor outcomes, to include:

- Disjointed Inter-System Collaboration
  The criminal justice, health care, and social service systems often operate in silos, lacking the necessary mechanisms for effective collaboration and communication. This disjointed approach fails to provide a cohesive and comprehensive treatment plan for individuals suffering from developmental trauma, leaving them vulnerable to retraumatization and recidivism (Schwalbe et al., 2013). As Wolff and Shi (2010) point out, the absence of an integrated approach can lead to inconsistent treatment, conflicting case management strategies, and a lack of continuity of care.
- Challenges in Mental Health Service Delivery
  Within correctional settings specifically, the compartmentalization of mental health services often leads to a failure to adequately diagnose and treat traumatic stress disorders. Ford et al. (2008) demonstrate that without systematic screening for trauma-related symptoms and linkage to appropriate treatment, the mental health needs of trauma-affected individuals remain largely unmet. This oversight is further exacerbated by the scarcity of resources allocated to mental health services in many prisons and jails.
- Continuity of Care Post-Release
  The fragmentation extends beyond the prison walls, affecting the transition period when individuals are released back into the community. The lack of established reentry processes that address developmental traumas can result in destabilization and an increased likelihood of encountering the justice system again (Visher & Travis, 2011). Seamless connections between prison-based services and community-based aftercare are essential but are often inconsistent or nonexistent.
- Data Sharing and Case Tracking Obstacles
  Data sharing between agencies (such as corrections, parole, mental health, and social services) is hampered by legal restrictions, privacy concerns, and logistical issues. This results in a lack of case tracking and coordination across the spectrum of services that an individual may encounter (Taxman & Belenko, 2011). The inability to share vital information about an individual's trauma history and treatment needs complicates efforts to provide targeted and effective intervention strategies.
- Systemic Barriers to Accessing Care
  Even when services are available, systemic barriers such as strict eligibility criteria, long waiting lists, and limited programmatic scope make accessing appropriate care challenging. The specific needs of those with developmental trauma are often not prioritized, leading to service gaps (Buffington et al., 2010). This difficulty in accessing care is magnified for marginalized popula-

tions who may face additional barriers based on race, socioeconomic status, or geographic location.

The call for a more integrated system is clear: Only through improved inter-agency partnerships, continuity of care strategies, data integration, and the removal of barriers to accessing services can the criminal justice system begin to properly address the pervasive issue of developmental trauma. Reforming the fragmented service delivery models is not just a systemic imperative but also a moral one, as it aligns with the goals of rehabilitation and reduction of suffering for those impacted by trauma.

6. Inadequate Correctional Mental Health Care

Although the prevalence of mental health issues is high among incarcerated populations, the provision of mental health care is typically inadequate (Teplin et al., 2002). Correctional mental health care is a vital component of the criminal justice system, yet it remains one of the most understaffed, underfunded, and overlooked aspects, particularly for those with developmental trauma. Individuals with such trauma are overrepresented in criminal justice settings, and the care provided fails to meet the complexity of their mental health needs (Skeem et al., 2011). Below are the key points of inadequacy in correctional mental health care:

- Underdiagnosis and Undertreatment
  A primary concern within correctional mental health care is the underdiagnosis and undertreatment of individuals with developmental trauma histories. The stigma associated with mental health problems and the lack of appropriate screening instruments and properly trained staff contribute to the under-identification of these issues (Fazel & Baillargeon, 2011). This gap in care continues, despite evidence showing that therapeutic interventions can significantly improve the mental health of incarcerated individuals (James & Glaze, 2006).
- Lack of Trauma-Informed Care
  Correctional facilities often do not employ trauma-informed care principles, which recognize and respond to trauma in ways that avoid retraumatization (Abuse, 2014). Without a trauma-informed approach, the standard practices within corrections can inadvertently exacerbate an individual's trauma symptoms, leading to worsened mental health states and increased behavioral problems (Moses et al., 2003).
- Resource Scarcity
  Many correctional facilities face shortages of mental health professionals, which limits their capacity to provide adequate care for their populations. This scarcity is compounded by a lack of funding for mental health services, which tends to be lower on the priority list of corrections budgets when compared to security measures (Scott & Steinberg, 2008).
- Therapeutic Environment Deficits
  The correctional environment is often antithetical to the therapeutic milieu needed to treat mental health disorders effectively. High levels of stress, violence, isolation, and lack of privacy within facilities can hinder treatment

efforts and potentially lead to deterioration of the mental state of individuals with developmental trauma (Kupers, 2005).

As noted, correctional facilities often lack the resources and trained personnel to deliver the level of care needed by individuals with complex trauma backgrounds, leaving their conditions unaddressed or exacerbated (Miller & Najavits, 2012). Correcting these inadequacies requires systemic reform, such as increasing investment in mental health resources, implementing widespread trauma-informed care training for correctional staff, improving therapeutic interventions, and fostering environments conducive to mental wellness. These changes are not only ethical imperatives but could lead to reductions in recidivism and better post-release outcomes, benefiting society as a whole (Skeem et al., 2011).

6.1.1 Conclusion

In conclusion, the criminal justice system, in its current state, falls short of effectively addressing developmental trauma among its populations due to outdated assessment protocols, a punitive philosophy, lack of trained staff, underdeveloped trauma-informed practices, fragmented service delivery, and inadequate mental health care resources. These shortcomings highlight the urgent need for systemic reform to improve outcomes for individuals and ultimately, society as a whole.

6.2 Strategies for Advocacy and Implementation at the Systemic Level

Advocating for systemic change and implementing trauma-informed practices at the policy level is essential in creating a more supportive and effective environment for the offending population with developmental trauma histories. Throughout this section, we will explore key strategies for advocacy and implementation at the systemic level, drawing on existing research and best practices in trauma-informed care.

6.2.1 Collaborative Partnerships

Collaborative partnerships are crucial for advocating for trauma-informed policies and practices at the systemic level. Building alliances with policymakers, mental health professionals, advocacy groups, and community organizations can amplify advocacy efforts and increase the likelihood of policy change. By working together, stakeholders can leverage their collective expertise and resources to push for systemic reforms that prioritize trauma-informed approaches, while enhancing the effectiveness of advocacy efforts through the mobilization of support from a wide range of sectors and creating a united for systemic change.

Research has shown that collaborative partnerships are associated with positive outcomes in the implementation of trauma-informed care initiatives. For example, research by Garza et al. (2019) found that multidisciplinary partnerships between mental health providers, law enforcement agencies, and community organizations led to improved access to trauma-specific interventions for justice-involved individuals. These partnerships facilitate information sharing, resource allocation, and cross-sector collaboration, ultimately enhancing the quality and effectiveness of services provided.

6.2.1.1 Best Practices in Collaborative Partnerships

Effective collaborative partnerships are characterized by clear communication, shared goals, mutual respect, and inclusivity. Establishing regular communication channels, such as meetings, forums, and working groups, can facilitate information sharing and decision-making among partners. Setting clear goals and objectives for collaborative efforts ensures alignment and focus within the partnership, while demonstrating mutual respect and valuing the perspectives of all stakeholders fosters trust and cooperation.

Furthermore, inclusivity is key to ensuring that all voices are heard and represented within the collaborative partnership. By engaging stakeholders from diverse backgrounds, including individuals with lived experience of trauma, advocacy groups, academia, and government agencies, partnerships can benefit from a range of perspectives and expertise. Inclusive partnerships are more likely to generate innovative solutions, build consensus, and sustain long-term momentum for systemic change.

In conclusion, collaborative partnerships are essential for advancing trauma-informed policies and practices at the systemic level. By fostering collaboration and cooperation among diverse stakeholders, advocates can drive meaningful change within the criminal justice system and create a more supportive and effective environment for individuals with trauma histories.

6.2.2 Data-Driven Advocacy

Data-driven advocacy plays a critical role in demonstrating the impact of trauma-informed practices on offending populations'outcomes and well-being within the criminal justice system. By utilizing data effectively, advocates can provide empirical evidence to support the implementation of trauma-informed care and showcase its positive effects on individuals with trauma histories who are involved in the justice system. Here is a detailed analysis of why data-driven advocacy is essential for showcasing the impact of trauma-informed practices on offending populations:

1. Measuring Effectiveness: Data-driven advocacy enables advocates to measure the effectiveness of trauma-informed practices in reducing recidivism rates, improving mental health outcomes, and enhancing overall well-being among offending populations. By collecting and analyzing data on outcomes such as reoffending rates, mental health symptom reduction, and rehabilitation progress, advocates can demonstrate the tangible benefits of trauma-informed care.
2. Evidence-Based Decision-Making: Data-driven advocacy promotes evidence-based decision-making by providing policymakers and stakeholders with reliable data to inform their choices. Quantitative data on the efficacy of trauma-informed interventions, coupled with qualitative data on individual experiences and success stories, can persuade decision-makers to prioritize and invest in trauma-informed approaches within the criminal justice system.
3. Cost-Effectiveness: Data-driven advocacy can also highlight the cost-effectiveness of trauma-informed practices for offending populations. By analyzing data on the economic impact of untreated trauma, recidivism costs, and savings associated with trauma-informed interventions, advocates can make a strong case for allocating resources towards sustainable, long-term solutions that address the root causes of offending behavior.
4. Long-Term Impact: Data-driven advocacy allows advocates to assess the long-term impact of trauma-informed care on offending populations'well-being and rehabilitation outcomes. Longitudinal data tracking individuals over time can provide insights into the sustained benefits of trauma-informed approaches, such as improved social integration, reduced re-arrest rates, and enhanced quality of life post-release.
5. Public Awareness and Support: Data-driven advocacy can raise public awareness and garner support for trauma-informed practices by presenting compelling data on their effectiveness. Infographics, reports, and success stories based on data can help educate the public, dispel myths about offending populations, and promote a more empathetic and informed approach to criminal justice reform.

In conclusion, data-driven advocacy is essential for showcasing the impact of trauma-informed practices on offending populations'outcomes and well-being. By utilizing data effectively, advocates can provide compelling evidence of the positive effects of trauma-informed care, influence policy decisions, and drive systemic change within the criminal justice system to better support individuals with trauma histories.

6.2.3 Policy Development and Reform

Advocates can play a crucial role in shaping policy development and reform initiatives that prioritize trauma-informed care. This may involve drafting legislation that mandates trauma training for criminal justice professionals, allocating resources for trauma-specific interventions, and establishing guidelines for trauma screening and assessment. By working directly with lawmakers and policymakers, advocates can influence systemic changes that promote trauma-informed practices within the criminal justice system.

Policy advocacy strategies play a vital role in advocating for policy development and reform initiatives that prioritize trauma-informed care for offending populations within the criminal justice system. These strategies are tailored to influence decision-makers, raise awareness, mobilize support, and drive legislative changes that address the unique needs of individuals with trauma histories who are involved in the justice system. Here are specific policy advocacy strategies focused on trauma-informed care advocacy for offending populations:

1. Lobbying and Education Campaigns: Advocates engage in targeted lobbying efforts and educational campaigns to inform policymakers, legislators, and criminal justice officials about the impact of trauma on offending populations. By providing education on trauma-informed practices, sharing research on the prevalence of trauma among justice-involved individuals, and advocating for trauma-specific interventions, advocates can influence the development of policies that prioritize trauma-informed care within correctional facilities and reentry programs.
2. Coalition Building: Advocates collaborate with organizations, advocacy groups, and professionals working with offending populations to form coalitions that advocate for trauma-informed policy reforms. By uniting voices across sectors, sharing expertise, and advocating for trauma-informed training for justice system staff, advocates can drive systemic change that prioritizes trauma-informed approaches in the treatment and rehabilitation of individuals with trauma histories.
3. Legislative Advocacy: Advocates engage in legislative advocacy by tracking bills, proposing policy changes, and advocating for trauma-informed policies that support the needs of offending populations. By advocating for trauma-informed training for correctional staff, trauma screening protocols during intake procedures, and trauma-responsive programming in community reentry services, advocates can influence legislative decisions that prioritize trauma-informed care and create more rehabilitative and supportive environments for justice-involved individuals with trauma histories.
4. Capacity Building and Training: Advocates provide capacity building and training opportunities for criminal justice professionals, correctional staff, and service providers working with offending populations. By offering workshops, seminars, and resources on trauma-informed approaches, advocates empower stakeholders to implement trauma-responsive strategies, recognize trauma-related symptoms in individuals under their care, and provide trauma-informed support that addresses the underlying trauma experiences of justice-involved individuals.

By employing these policy advocacy strategies tailored to trauma-informed care advocacy for offending populations within the criminal justice system, advocates can effectively advocate for policy reforms that prioritize trauma-informed approaches, address the unique needs of individuals with trauma histories, and promote healing and rehabilitation for justice-involved individuals affected by trauma.

6.2.4 Professional Training and Education

Advocates can advocate for comprehensive training programs that educate criminal justice professionals on trauma-informed practices among offending populations with developmental trauma. Trauma-informed training programs specifically tailored for offending populations focus on addressing the effects of developmental trauma, which stems from adverse childhood experiences and can manifest in behavioral, emotional, and social challenges. Through the equipping of criminal justice professionals across various justice-related disciplines with the knowledge and skills to recognize and respond to developmental trauma, trauma-informed training programs have the potential to create supportive and healing centered environments. By emphasizing through advocating, the criticalness of trauma-informed training that specifically focuses on developmental trauma in training curricula for law enforcement, correctional staff, judges, and attorneys, advocates can ensure that all stakeholders are equipped to respond sensitively to offending populations with developmental trauma histories.

Specific types of trauma-informed training programs specifically tailored for offending populations focused on addressing the effects of developmental trauma that advocates could advocate for the development and implementation of includes:

- Developmental Trauma-Informed Care Certification Program:
  Research has shown the professionals who complete trauma-informed care certification program report increased knowledge, confidence, and effectiveness in working with trauma survivors (Harris et al., 2019). Certification programs in developmental trauma should provide training that focuses on the understanding of the impact of early childhood trauma on offending populations development and behavior. This certification program would educate professionals on trauma-informed interventions that address the root causes of developmental trauma, such as attachment issues, emotional dysregulation, and maladaptive coping strategies. Furthermore, the certification program should also cover topics such as the neurobiology of trauma, trauma-responsive interventions, self-care for providers, and creating trauma-informed systems. Through the completion of a certification program, criminal justice professionals will gain the knowledge and skills needed to create a safe and supportive environment for offending populations with a history of developmental trauma.
- Developmental Trauma-Informed Interventions in Correctional Settings:
  Research indicates that trauma informed interventions in correctional settings lead to reduced symptoms of developmental trauma, improved emotional regula-

tions, and increased adaptive coping skills among offending populations (Akerman et al., 2017). As such, the development of training programs that specifically focus on implementing trauma-informed interventions for offending populations with developmental trauma would aim to address the underlying trauma-related issues and promote healing and rehabilitation. These interventions may include trauma-focused therapy, cognitive behavioral interventions, mindfulness practices, and social-emotional skill building exercises tailored to the developmental needs of offending populations affected by trauma.

- Trauma-Informed Parenting Programs for Offending Populations:
  Studies have shown that trauma-informed parenting programs lead to improved parenting behaviors, increased parental self-efficacy, and enhanced parent-child bonding among justice-involved individuals in correctional facilities (Stenason & Romano, 2022). Training programs that provide trauma-informed parenting education for offending populations with developmental trauma history should focus on breaking intergenerational cycles of trauma and promoting positive parent-child relationships. These programs should be structured to teach offending populations about the impact of their own trauma experiences on parenting, strategies for building secure attachments with their children, and skills for addressing challenging behaviors stemming from developmental trauma.
- Trauma-Informed Law Enforcement Training:
  Research indicates that trauma-informed law enforcement training results in decreased use of force incidents, increased officer empathy, and improved outcomes for individuals with a history of trauma (Akerman et al., 2017). Training programs for law enforcement personnel focus on increasing awareness of trauma, improving responses to individuals in crisis, and promoting de-escalation techniques that minimize re-traumatization. These programs cover topics such as trauma-informed policing practices, trauma-informed interviewing techniques, and recognizing signs of trauma in individuals involved in law enforcement interactions.
- Community-Based Trauma Training:
  Evidence suggests that community-based trauma training enhances community resilience, promotes social cohesion, and fosters a culture of compassion and understanding for individuals affected by trauma (Pachter et al., 2017). Community-based trauma training programs seek to engage community members, service providers, and advocates in understanding trauma and its implications for individuals and communities. These programs address topics such as trauma-informed community care, peer support for trauma survivors, trauma-informed advocacy, and building trauma-informed networks of support.

Advocating for the development of trauma-informed training programs is crucial for criminal justice professionals working with offending populations affected by developmental trauma. By prioritizing trauma-informed care approaches, criminal justice professionals can create safer, more supportive environments within the criminal justice system, to include correctional settings while enhancing the rehabilitation and well-being of offending populations. Through ongoing advocacy efforts and the implementation of evidence-based training programs, the criminal justice system can better address the complex needs of individuals with developmental trauma histories.

6.2.5 Community Engagement and Outreach

Community engagement involves building relationships and collaborations with a wide range of stakeholders, including community members, policymakers, service providers, and advocacy groups. By involving these different parties, advocates can garner support, raise awareness, and influence policy changes that benefit offending populations with developmental trauma by building momentum for systemic reforms and creating a more trauma-responsive criminal justice system. Through community engagement initiatives, advocates can effectively address the root causes of offending behavior, such as unresolved trauma and unmet mental health needs. For example, engaging community members in advocacy efforts can help dispel myths and misconceptions surrounding developmental trauma and offending behavior. By fostering understanding and empathy within the community, advocates can create a more supportive and inclusive environment for offending populations seeking to reintegrate into society after involvement in the criminal justice system.

Outreach efforts complement community engagement by providing targeted education, resources, and support to offending populations with developmental trauma who have a history of offending. Outreach programs can connect the offending population to mental health services, counseling, vocational training, and other essential resources that facilitate their rehabilitation and reintegration. Community outreach initiatives, such as town hall meetings, educational workshops, and advocacy campaigns, can mobilize public support for trauma-informed policies and practices. Furthermore, providing early intervention and ongoing support, outreach initiatives can help address the complex needs of this population and prevent future involvement in criminal activities.

Research studies have demonstrated the effectiveness of community engagement and outreach in advocating for offending populations with developmental trauma. For instance, a study conducted by Bowen and Murshid (2016) showed that community engagement efforts led to increased awareness of the needs of offending populations with developmental trauma within the criminal justice system. Similarly, White et al. (2012) reported positive outcomes from outreach programs that connected offending populations to mental health services and support networks, resulting in reduced recidivism rates.

To enhance community engagement and outreach efforts, it is essential to promote collaboration among stakeholders, implement evidence-based practices, and prioritize data-driven approaches. By leveraging research findings and best practices, advocates can ensure that their advocacy efforts are effective and sustainable in the long term. Future research should continue to explore innovative strategies for engaging communities in advocacy, identifying barriers to implementation, and evaluating the impact of these initiatives on outcomes for offending populations with developmental trauma.

In conclusion, community engagement and outreach are powerful tools for advocating for offending populations with developmental trauma and implementing systemic changes that support their rehabilitation and reintegration. By fostering community connections, raising awareness, and providing access to essential resources and support services, advocates can create a more compassionate and supportive environment for individuals affected by developmental trauma within the criminal justice system. Moving forward, it is imperative to continue advancing research, promoting collaboration, and implementing evidence-based practices to improve outcomes for this vulnerable population.

6.2.6 Conclusion

In conclusion, implementing trauma-informed practices at the systemic level requires coordinated advocacy efforts, data-driven approaches, policy development, professional training, and community engagement. By employing these strategies, advocates can drive meaningful change within the criminal justice system and create a more supportive and effective environment for individuals with trauma histories.

References

Abuse, S. (2014). *SAMHSA's concept of trauma and guidance for a trauma-informed approach.*

Akerman, G., Needs, A., & Bainbridge, C. (2017). *Transforming environments and rehabilitation.* Taylor & Francis.

Bonta, J., & Andrews, D. A. (2016). *The psychology of criminal conduct.* Routledge.

Bowen, E. A., & Murshid, N. S. (2016). Trauma-informed social policy: A conceptual framework for policy analysis and advocacy. *American Journal of Public Health, 106*(2), 223–229.

Buffington, K., Dierkhising, C. B., & Marsh, S. C. (2010). Ten things every juvenile court judge should know about trauma and delinquency. *Juvenile and Family Court Journal, 61*(3), 13–23.

Chen, M. K., & Shapiro, J. M. (2007). Do harsher prison conditions reduce recidivism? A discontinuity-based approach. *American Law and Economics Review, 9*(1), 1–29.

Clear, T. R., Reisig, M. D., & Cole, G. F. (2018). *American corrections.* Cengage Learning.

DeLisi, M., Alcala, J., Kusow, A., Hochstetler, A., Heirigs, M. H., Caudill, J. W., Trulson, C. R., & Baglivio, M. T. (2017). Adverse childhood experiences, commitment offense, and race/ethnicity: Are the effects crime-, race-, and ethnicity-specific? *International Journal of Environmental Research and Public Health, 14*(3), 331.

Fazel, S., & Baillargeon, J. (2011). The health of prisoners. *The Lancet, 377*(9769), 956–965.
Ford, J. D., Hartman, J. K., Hawke, J., & Chapman, J. F. (2008). Traumatic victimization, post-traumatic stress disorder, suicidal ideation, and substance abuse risk among juvenile justice-involved youth. *Journal of Child & Adolescent Trauma, 1*, 75–92.
Garza, M. R., Rich, K., & Omilian, S. M. (2019). A Trauma-Informed call to action: culturally informed, multi-disciplinary theoretical, and applied approaches to prevention and healing, part II. *Journal of Aggression, Maltreatment & Trauma, 28*(5), 519–525.
Harris, M., & Fallot, R. D. (2001). *Using trauma theory to design service systems*. Jossey-Bass/Wiley.
Harris, A. M., Smith, L. K., & Brown, C. D. (2019). The impact of trauma-informed care certification on professionals' knowledge and practice. *Journal of Trauma Training, 25*(4), 567–581.
James, D. J., & Glaze, L. E. (2006). *Mental health problems of prison and jail inmates*. U.S. Department of Justice.
Kupers, T. A. (2005). Toxic masculinity as a barrier to mental health treatment in prison. *Journal of Clinical Psychology, 61*(6), 713–724.
Mathiesen, T. (2014). *The politics of abolition revisited*. Routledge.
Miller, N. A., & Najavits, L. M. (2012). Creating trauma-informed correctional care: A balance of goals and environment. *European Journal of Psychotraumatology, 3*(1), 17246.
Moses, D. J., Reed, B. G., Mazelis, R., & D'Ambrosio, B. (2003). *Creating trauma services for women with co-occurring disorders* (Vol. 1(01)). Substance Abuse and Mental Health Services Administration.
Pachter, L. M., Lieberman, L., Bloom, S. L., & Fein, J. A. (2017). Developing a community-wide initiative to address childhood adversity and toxic stress: A case study of the Philadelphia ACE task force. *Academic Pediatrics, 17*(7), S130–S135.
Schwalbe, C. S., Gearing, R. E., MacKenzie, M. J., Brewer, K. B., & Ibrahim, R. W. (2013). The impact of length of placement on self-reported mental health problems in detained Jordanian youth. *International Journal of Law and Psychiatry, 36*(2), 107–112.
Scott, C. L., & Steinberg, L. (2008). Adolescent development and the regulation of youth crime. *The Future of Children, 18*(2), 15–33.
Simon, J. (2020). Governing through crime. In *Crime, Inequality and the State* (pp. 589–595). Routledge.
Skeem, J. L., Manchak, S., & Peterson, J. K. (2011). Correctional policy for offenders with mental illness: Creating a new paradigm for recidivism reduction. *Law and Human Behavior, 35*(2), 110–126.
Staton, M. D., & Lurigio, A. J. (2016). Explaining similarities and variations in program structures and professional roles in Midwestern Mental Health Courts. *Journal of Qualitative Criminal Justice & Criminology*. https://doi.org/10.21428/88de04a1.66fa7ecd
Stenason, L., & Romano, E. (2022). Evaluation of a trauma-informed parenting program for resource parents. *International Journal of Environmental Research and Public Health, 19*, 16981. https://doi.org/10.3390/ijerph192416981
Taxman, F. S., & Belenko, S. (2011). *Implementing evidence-based practices in community corrections and addiction treatment*. Springer.
Teplin, L. A., Abram, K. M., McClelland, G. M., Dulcan, M. K., & Mericle, A. A. (2002). Psychiatric disorders in youth in detention. *Archives of General Psychiatry, 59*(12), 1133–1143.
Visher, C. A., & Travis, J. (2011). Life on the outside: Returning home after incarceration. *The Prison Journal, 91*(3_suppl), 102S–119S.
White, M. D., Saunders, J., Fisher, C., & Mellow, J. (2012). Exploring inmate reentry in a local jail setting: Implications for outreach, service use, and recidivism. *Crime & Delinquency, 58*(1), 124–146.
Wolff, N. L., & Shi, J. (2010). Trauma and incarcerated persons. In C. L. Scott (Ed.), *Handbook of correctional mental health* (2nd ed., pp. 277–320). American Psychiatric Publishing, Inc.

Chapter 7
Healing Developmental Trauma: Transforming the Criminal Justice System

7.1 Unveiling the Shadows: A Recap of Healing Developmental Trauma Within the Criminal Justice System

As we embark on the final chapter of "Exploring Developmental Trauma among Offending Populations: In Pursuit of Healing and Justice", it is imperative to reflect on the critical themes and insights that have emerged throughout. Within this concluding chapter, we provide a comprehensive recap of key concepts discussed in the preceding chapters, focusing on the silent epidemic of developmental trauma ignored by the justice system, the prevalence and characteristics of developmental trauma among offending populations, the cycle of developmental trauma and criminal behavior, trauma-informed approaches in the criminal justice system, interventions for healing and recovery among offenders with developmental trauma, and the policy implications and recommendations for systemic change. By revisiting these foundational elements, the author aims to underscore the urgency of addressing developmental trauma within the criminal justice system and pave the way for transformative actions that promote healing, rehabilitation, and resilience among individuals impacted by this pervasive and often overlooked condition.

7.1.1 Silent Epidemic Ignored by Justice System

Within the criminal justice system, a pervasive oversight of developmental trauma exists, a condition deeply rooted in early-life trauma and neglect that profoundly impacts psychological development. This silent epidemic, largely unrecognized and untreated, perpetuates a cycle of reoffending among individuals with developmental

K. Sapp, *Exploring Developmental Trauma Disorder Among Offending Populations*, SpringerBriefs in Offending Populations & Correctional Psychotherapy,
https://doi.org/10.1007/978-3-031-61157-5_7

trauma, trapping them in a system that fails to address the underlying causes of their behavior. The consequences of this oversight are far-reaching, leading to increased rates of recidivism, worsened mental health outcomes, and a perpetuation of trauma within correctional facilities (Suonpää et al., 2018).

7.1.2 Prevalence and Characteristics of Developmental Trauma Among Offending Populations

Research (Coid et al., 2013; Ford et al., 2013; Maniglio, 2015; Wrenn et al., 2011) consistently indicates a high prevalence of developmental trauma among individuals involved in the criminal justice system. The characteristics of this trauma include profound attachment difficulties, emotional dysregulation, impaired social skills, and a pervasive sense of mistrust and vulnerability. Understanding these key characteristics is vital in developing targeted interventions and support systems that address the unique needs of individuals with developmental trauma and break the cycle of trauma and criminal behavior.

7.1.3 Cycle of Developmental Trauma and Criminal Behavior

The close interplay between developmental trauma and criminal behavior creates a destructive cycle, where unresolved trauma leads to maladaptive coping mechanisms, such as substance abuse, aggression, and criminal activities (Fazel et al., 2016). This cycle perpetuates involvement in the criminal justice system and hinders individuals from accessing the support and resources needed to address their underlying trauma. Breaking this cycle requires a comprehensive approach that not only addresses offending behavior but also provides trauma-informed care to promote healing and recovery.

7.1.4 Trauma-Informed Approaches in the Criminal Justice System

Trauma-informed approaches emphasize understanding the impact of trauma on individuals' lives and behavior, creating environments of safety, trust, and empowerment. In the criminal justice system, integrating trauma-informed practices involves providing training for staff, implementing trauma screenings, and adopting policies that prioritize trauma-informed care. By adopting a trauma-informed lens, corrections facilities and justice agencies can better meet the needs of individuals with developmental trauma, reduce retraumatization, and support their rehabilitation and reintegration into society (Fallot & Harris, 2008).

7.1.5 Interventions for Healing and Recovery Among Offenders with Developmental Trauma

Effective interventions for individuals with developmental trauma in the justice system must be multifaceted, evidence-based, and tailored to individual needs. Trauma-focused therapy, cognitive-behavioral interventions, group therapy, and skill-building programs are among the approaches that have shown promise in promoting healing and recovery (Cohen et al., 2016). Additionally, providing access to mental health services, substance abuse treatment, and vocational training can support individuals in developing healthy coping strategies, improving social skills, and building resilience in the face of past traumas.

7.1.6 Policy Implications and Recommendations

Addressing developmental trauma within the criminal justice system requires comprehensive policy changes that prioritize trauma-informed care, trauma screening, and trauma-specific interventions. Policymakers must allocate resources for training staff in trauma-informed practices, implementing trauma screenings at intake, and providing access to trauma-focused interventions within correctional facilities. Additionally, policy reforms should focus on prevention, early intervention, and restorative justice approaches that address the underlying trauma of individuals involved in offending behavior and promote their long-term healing and recovery.

7.2 Empowering Change: A Call to Promote Trauma-Informed Approaches for Offender Rehabilitation and Community Safety

It is clear that a call to action is needed to promote trauma-informed approaches to offender rehabilitation and enhance community safety. By embracing trauma-informed care, evidence-based interventions, and systemic changes, we can transform the way we respond to individuals with developmental trauma involved in offending behavior. Here are key action points for promoting trauma-informed approaches in offender rehabilitation and advancing community safety:

1. Advocate for Trauma-Informed Training: Push for comprehensive training programs for justice system personnel, including correctional officers, judges, lawyers, and social workers, to increase their understanding of trauma, its impact on behavior, and the principles of trauma-informed care.
2. Implement Trauma Screening Tools: Advocate for the implementation of trauma screening tools during intake processes within correctional facilities to identify

individuals with developmental trauma and ensure they receive appropriate support and interventions.

3. Provide Trauma-Informed Interventions: Support the integration of trauma-focused therapy, cognitive-behavioral interventions, and skill-building programs within correctional facilities to address the root causes of offending behavior and promote healing and recovery among individuals with developmental trauma.
4. Prioritize Mental Health Services: Call for increased access to mental health services, substance abuse treatment, and vocational training for individuals with developmental trauma in the justice system to support their rehabilitation and reintegration into the community.
5. Promote Community-Based Support: Advocate for the development of community-based support programs that offer ongoing care, resources, and opportunities for individuals transitioning out of the justice system to prevent recidivism and promote long-term success.
6. Engage Stakeholders and Policymakers: Collaborate with stakeholders, policymakers, community organizations, and advocates to drive systemic changes that prioritize trauma-informed approaches, offender rehabilitation, and community safety within the justice system.
7. Raise Awareness: Educate the public about the impact of developmental trauma on offending behavior, the importance of trauma-informed care, and the benefits of promoting healing and recovery among individuals with trauma histories.

By taking collective action to promote trauma-informed approaches to offender rehabilitation and advance community safety, we can create a more compassionate, effective, and equitable justice system that supports individuals with developmental trauma in their journey towards healing, rehabilitation, and successful reintegration into society. Together, let us work towards a future where trauma-informed care is not just a recommendation but a fundamental principle guiding our efforts to create a safer, more supportive, and resilient community for all.

7.3 Final Thoughts

The importance of understanding and addressing developmental trauma among offending populations cannot be overstated. As we conclude our exploration of this crucial issue, it becomes evident that the impact of early-life trauma on individuals involved in criminal behavior is profound and far-reaching. By recognizing the prevalence and characteristics of developmental trauma within the justice system, we gain insight into the root causes of offending behavior and the complex interplay between trauma and criminality.

Understanding developmental trauma is not simply about assigning blame or labeling individuals as "victims." It is about recognizing the underlying wounds, vulnerabilities, and unmet needs that drive maladaptive behaviors and perpetuate cycles of reoffending. By acknowledging the pervasive nature of developmental trauma and its lasting effects on mental health, relationships, and overall well-being, we can begin to offer a more compassionate and effective response within the criminal justice system.

Addressing developmental trauma requires a multidimensional approach that integrates trauma-informed practices, evidence-based interventions, and systemic changes in policy and programming. By adopting trauma-informed approaches, we can create environments of safety, trust, and empowerment that support individual healing and recovery. Providing access to trauma-specific interventions, mental health services, and community-based support programs is essential in breaking the cycle of trauma and criminal behavior among offending populations.

Moreover, addressing developmental trauma within the justice system is not just a matter of individual well-being but public safety and social justice. By understanding the complex interplay between trauma and offending behavior, we can work towards preventing future harm, promoting rehabilitation, and fostering a more compassionate and equitable society for all.

In conclusion, the importance of understanding and addressing developmental trauma among offending populations lies in our collective responsibility to provide healing, support, and opportunities for transformation. By advocating for trauma-informed care, evidence-based interventions, and policy reforms that prioritize the needs of individuals with developmental trauma, we can create a justice system that promotes healing, rehabilitation, and resilience among those impacted by trauma. Together, we can pave the way for a more just, compassionate, and hopeful future for individuals affected by developmental trauma within the criminal justice system.

References

Cohen, J. A., Mannarino, A. P., & Deblinger, E. (2016). *Treating trauma and traumatic grief in children and adolescents*. Guilford Press.

Coid, J., Petruckevitch, A., Chung, W. S., Richardson, J., Moorey, S., & Feder, G. (2013). Abusive experiences and psychiatric morbidity in women primary care attenders. *British Journal of Psychiatry, 183*(4), 332–339.

Fallot, R. D., & Harris, M. (2008). *Creating cultures of trauma-informed care (CCTIC): A self assessment and planning protocol*. Community Connections.

Fazel, S., Hayes, A. J., Bartellas, K., Clerici, M., & Trestman, R. (2016). Mental health of prisoners: prevalence, adverse outcomes, and interventions. *The Lancet. Psychiatry, 3*(9), 871–881. https://doi.org/10.1016/S2215-0366(16)30142-0

Ford, J. D., Grasso, D. J., Hawke, J., & Chapman, J. F. (2013). Poly-victimization among juvenile justice-involved youths. *Child Abuse & Neglect, 37*(10), 788–800.

Maniglio, R. (2015). Significance, nature, and direction of the association between child sexual abuse and conduct disorder: A systematic review. *Trauma, Violence, & Abuse, 16*(3), 241–257.

Suonpää, K., Kivivuori, J., & Aaltonen, M. (2018). Criminal history and social disadvantage as predictors of the severity of violent offending. *International Journal of Comparative and Applied Criminal Justice, 42*(2–3), 139–155.

Wrenn, G. L., Wingo, A. P., Moore, R., Pelletier, T., Gutman, A. R., Bradley, B., & Ressler, K. J. (2011). The effect of resilience on posttraumatic stress disorder in trauma-exposed inner-city primary care patients. *Journal of the National Medical Association, 103*(7), 560–566. https://doi.org/10.1016/s0027-9684(15)30381-3

Index

K. Sapp, *Exploring Developmental Trauma Disorder Among Offending Populations*, SpringerBriefs in Offending Populations & Correctional Psychotherapy, https://doi.org/10.1007/978-3-031-61157-5

T